KNOW YOUR CAT

FRANCESCA RICCOMINI

KNOW YOUR
CAT
UNDERSTAND HOW YOUR
CAT THINKS AND BEHAVES

FALL RIVER PRESS

Fall River Press
122 Fifth Avenue
New York, NY 10011

ISBN: 978-1-4351-1384-8

Printed and bound in China

10 9 8 7 6 5 4 3 2 1

Note
The advice in this book is provided as general information only.
It is not necessarily specific to any individual case and is not a
substitute for the guidance and advice provided by a licensed
veterinary practitioner consulted in any particular situation.
Octopus Publishing Group accepts no liability or responsibility
for any consequences resulting from the use of or reliance upon
the information contained herein.

No cats or kittens were harmed in the making of this book.

Contents

Introduction

Cats are increasing in popularity in many parts of the world. Widely regarded as independent, self-reliant and less demanding than dogs, but nevertheless rewarding and entertaining companions, they are perceived as the ideal pet for busy people. To their credit, they frequently manage to fit into our homes with apparent ease. So well do they appear to cope with us humans and our foibles that it's easy to overlook the fact that they are animals. They share our homes, add joy to our lives and take part in our activities, but still they think, feel and act like the successful predators they are. This is all too easy to overlook in the way we care for them, and we often undermine their wellbeing when we treat our pet cats as little humans. Doing so too frequently can lead to problem behaviour that strains relationships with even the most treasured of pets.

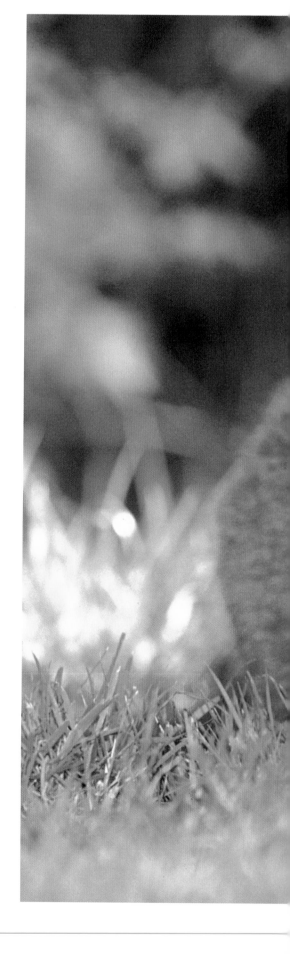

Right: Understanding your feline friend will ensure a happy, contented cat who will be a rewarding companion and family member.

Where do cats come from?

If you are to keep your cat happy, you must make sure that your expectations of him are realistic and fair. You will only do this if you understand the basis of his fascinating, and sometimes perplexing, behaviour. Only when what your cat does becomes less puzzling will your chances of being a diligent, caring owner be improved, and only when you truly understand your cat will you be able to get the best out of him and derive even greater pleasure from the representative of *Felis silvestris catus* that condescends to live with you, allowing you to provide for and love him.

The first domesticated cats

To truly understand your cat you need to know a bit about where his forebears came from, and given that cats have been domesticated for so long it's surprising how much we still have to learn. However, studies of genetics, anatomy and coat colour have shown that the African wild cat (*Felis silvestris lybica*) is the original ancestor of our present-day felines.

All cats, from lions to your pet cat, belong to the family, *Felidae*, and within that family all the small cats, including yours, are classified as *Felis*. Other types of wild cat, *Felis silvestris*, the group to which your cat belongs, are the European wild cat (*F. silvestris silvestris*), the African wild cat (*F. silvestris lybica*), the Indian wild cat (*F. silvestris ornata*) and the domestic cat (*F. silvestris catus*). The exact process whereby cats were domesticated is still unclear, but when we look at our pets we see the descendants of the wild felids that roamed the African savannah.

The earliest evidence of cats co-habiting with man comes from a 9,500-year-old grave in Cyprus where a human and a cat were found buried together. However, we have the ancient Egyptians to thank for spotting the cats' potential as rodent controllers, when they noticed the small, lithe hunters in the newly established grain stores in the outskirts of their settlements. Later, the Romans introduced the domestic cat to the wider world (together with the concept of the lap dog).

It might seem that we've had plenty of time to influence the behaviour of our cats, but, unlike dogs, most cats have remained free to choose their mates themselves. In the same way, many have chosen to stay – or not – in individual homes ever since their ancestors came out of the desert to live with us.

It was only during the 20th century that people began to take a whole-hearted interest in the different types of cat that had developed in various areas of the world, and so began the serious business of breeding for specific physical and behavioural traits that has given rise to the range of pedigree breeds we have today. The end result is that, although people have cared for cats to a greater or lesser extent for centuries, until recently there has been little human interference with the characteristics and behaviour of these appealing creatures. With a few notable exceptions, they have remained relatively unchanged as they successfully navigated their way through all the hazards that nature and history have thrown at them.

This is why – if you want to really understand your cat, what he does and why – you need to know everything you can about the background of his ancestors, then you should look at:

- Where your pet was born
- What his parents were like
- What his first environment taught him about our world

It may sound somewhat farfetched to suggest that looking at the behaviour of cats that live in the desert or savannah, or live freely in our own society, can help explain what you observe your cat doing in his everyday life, but as you read on you could well be surprised.

The behaviours that enabled your cat's ancestors to survive and thrive in the wild are still there inside your pet, whether it's immediately obvious in all his daily activities or not. The more you understand where and why his species behaviour developed, the better chance you will have of knowing why he does what he does and when. The more you know your cat, the more able you will be to provide him with his ideal world. To do this, however, you will also need to understand why he is uniquely himself, which may make him very different from any other cat you've ever met, even his own family members. Genetic inheritance combines with life experiences and species characteristics to give us the range of feline personalities that bring owners so much pleasure.

This book will not only explain all the important aspects of your cat's behaviour but also the various influences that have shaped it. Its aim is to help you to 'know your cat'. As you read it, you may well find that in his own way he has rather subtly shaped your behaviour, too.

Left: Part of the fascination of feline behaviour is that the more we learn about the cats that share our lives, the more we realize we have yet to discover.

WHAT IS A CAT?

To answer this question we need to look briefly at where *Felis catus*, the cat, came from and his place in nature. Your cat's ancestor originally developed to survive in the conditions prevailing in its natural habitat, and although people might have 'taken the feline out of the desert', we haven't actually taken out of cats the features that allowed them to survive in that environment. In fact, our influence on the domestic cat has not been nearly as comprehensive as it might seem. So to help you get to know your cat, we will start by looking at how others of his kind stay safe and survive, pass on their genes, communicate effectively with each other and adapt to living alongside other cats and with us.

Hunter and hunted

Like us, cats are mammals. Unlike us, however, they are obligate carnivores, which means that they must eat meat. As a result, domestic cats are highly developed predators, and they come quite high up the food chain, small rodents and birds being their preferred prey.

The food chain

Sadly for those of us who value them, cats are also small enough to sometimes become a meal for larger carnivores (meat-eaters) and birds of prey. Being vulnerable in this way, as well as needing to be successful hunters, affects everything they do. Cats simply can't afford to take unnecessary risks or waste valuable energy, one of the reasons they are indeed champion sleepers.

In areas such as the desert, the natural environment of their ancestors, prey is thin on the ground, and the wild cat has evolved to live on the small creatures that also inhabit these places. These animals are too insubstantial to support a group of cats, so the cat remains a lone hunter. In addition, group involvement in a chase inevitably causes disturbance, which scares away the prey, while the solitary hunt is less likely to alert the prey so that it takes evasive action. The solitary cat's hunting technique is based on patience and stealth.

Survival skills

To be a successful individual hunter a cat needs to be able to detect its prey, then stalk, chase, pounce and capture it. Then, because even the smallest mouse, especially when fighting for its life, can inflict a nasty bite, to dispatch it in the least risky way possible. As a result, the feline senses of sight, hearing and scent are honed to perfection. Cats also have a remarkable ability to feel vibrations in the air with specially adapted hairs – the whiskers on their face and legs – and in the ground beneath their feet (see pages 14–17). These features, designed to help them locate the small creatures they live on, make cats seem almost supernaturally able to predict geological events, such as earthquakes. In fact, when you consider your cat's senses, the needs of his ancestors can still be clearly seen because everything about his body is designed to cope with the life his forebears led.

Food is only one requirement for any small feline living in a tough, hazardous environment. The wild cat's beautifully camouflaged tabby fur, kept sleek and glossy by frequent grooming, provides some protection from danger and the elements, and these amazing creatures can cope with extremes of searing daytime temperatures and intense chill at night.

The cat's anatomy, too, is superbly adapted for survival. Naturally lithe and sinuous, thanks to an especially flexible spine, the cat is designed for silent stalking, bursts of speed and abruptly launched attacks. The fore paws, with claws that grasp, are skilled at manipulation. The skull shape, jaws and teeth, will inflict a strong, effective killing bite and then the efficient tearing of the carcass.

Left: *The hunting skills that wild cats possess are also apparent in domesticated cats. Their highly-developed characteristics have been honed over many years of evolution.*

Below: *All the adaptations that allowed our cats' ancestors to survive in their environment of evolutionary adaptation (EEA) are still seen in our pets today.*

Feline senses

Cats are probably better known for their remarkable senses than most other aspects of their fascinating behaviour. Their eyes do indeed glow in the dark, and according to folklore they can predict earthquakes, balance on a tightrope and hear a pin drop six streets away. These claims may be somewhat exaggerated, but nevertheless your cat's sensory equipment is pretty impressive.

Everything works together

It's the combined information from all his senses that gives your cat his remarkable abilities. Although his ability to detect different tastes may be more limited and his sight different, rather than better, than ours, his acute sense of smell makes ours seem really rather feeble.

Paws and claws

Cats fore paws are well equipped with mechanoreceptors, which reflects their importance in hunting and manipulating food. You will notice this as your cat plays with objects if he's not a hunter. He may scoop up pawfuls of food before eating, or you may see him gaining information about surfaces by passing his paw over objects, something that leads some cats rather charmingly to 'play' with water.

However, cats are not the most dexterous animals. Raccoons, for example, have an even greater number of receptors and nerves associated with their paws, and they have even been trained to manipulate coins sufficiently well to pick them up and put them in piggy banks – until, that is, they decided they didn't want to relinquish them.

These receptors, also found on your cat's nose, occur in a highly specialized and sensitive form at the base of his claws. This may explain why many cats hate their feet being touched.

Whiskers

The long, stiff hairs found around the face and 'wrists' send important information to your cat's brain about the position of his head and legs in relation to nearby objects. Whiskers undoubtedly help him to move around in the dark or in confined spaces, but they are also sensitive to temperature and air movements.

Whiskers can also help convey your pet's mood to anyone who understands enough about feline body language to appreciate their movements. For example, when he is in danger your cat can flatten his whiskers out of harm's way. When he is investigating something he moves them forward, or he will stiffen and extend them sideways to make him look intimidating if he is confronting something threatening.

Hearing

Cats have remarkably mobile ears, which can move independently of each other. You've probably noticed this when your pet listens intently, trying to work out what's going on around him. This mobility, together with the ears' size and shape, helps your cat collect different sets of information from each side of his head. This is a skill of particular use when he's hunting at night because his ability to hear rustling in the undergrowth complements his dark-adapted sight, enabling him to locate rodents more effectively.

Above: By using the information he gleans from all his senses, your cat will keep track of everything that's going on around him.

Left: Cats have mechanoreceptors in their paws which they use to gather information on what they are touching.

At low sound frequencies (above 50 Hz) your cat probably hears much the same as you, but he comes into his own in the middle range frequencies, where his is one of the most sensitive of all mammalian species. In the higher range his hearing is slightly more effective than ours, but his ability to identify minute differences allows him to listen in on 'chats between mice' in a way we never could. If you're unfortunate enough to have the experience of mice coming into your house, you may only know it because your cat's concentrated listening behaviour tells you that there are small creatures moving around. This helps to explain why cat toys that squeak, as well as being light and quick moving, are most likely to engage your cat's attention.

TOUCH

When it comes to the important sense of touch, your cats' world is probably much the same as your own, although it's difficult to know exactly how they experience pain because it's such a subjective matter for humans. However, as we have similar anatomical structures in this respect, it is always more humane and ethical to err on the side of caution and assume that pain is as unpleasant for our pets as it is for us.

Like us, cats have receptor cells in their skin. These cells detect sensations and send information about them to the brain by way of what are known as the peripheral nerves. There are three types of receptor:

- Mechanoreceptors are sensitive to touch and pressure. There are two types: one is responsive to movements of the skin or hairs; the other is sensitive to displacement, such as that produced by sustained pressure on the pads.

- Thermoreceptors are sensitive to temperature, and there are different receptors for warmth and cold.

- Nociceptors are sensitive to pain.

Balance

Your cat's ears are not only concerned with detecting sound; they also help his balance. The particular sensitivity of what is known as the vestibular apparatus in your cat's inner ear is responsible, together with his remarkable flexibility, for his ability to balance and to right himself if he falls.

Sight

Your cat is a natural predator that hunts mainly at dawn and dusk, and his eyes are adapted to be especially effective in low-intensity light. Like us, he has binocular vision, although his eyes are set slightly further to the sides of his head than ours. One-eyed cats usually manage perfectly well after a period of adjustment to their sight loss, although they have to move their heads more to perceive depth than when they had two eyes.

We show more of the 'whites' of our eyes, which means that his are less mobile, but his pupils are able to contract and dilate more, which is why his can constrict to slits, both to protect his eyeball, which is comparatively larger than ours, and to communicate with others.

Cats are not the only mammals with a *tapetum lucidum*, a mirror-like reflective layer at the back of the eye, which causes the classic cats' eyes shining in the dark – seals have them too, for example. It increases the amount of light available for processing and improves the eye's efficiency by about 40 per cent, although in complete darkness cats are as helpless as their owners.

When it comes to detecting colour it's known that cats have some cones (the cells in the retina that detect colour), but it's thought that their brains don't process the information well

because colour has little meaning in the feline world, especially at night.

Adult cats tend to be short-sighted: their vision is best adapted to detect fast-moving prey more than 2 metres (about 6 feet) away. To detect objects near to them, they mainly rely on vibration via their whiskers and their hearing – you have probably observed this with your cat.

Taste

It is difficult to study cats' sense of taste, so we know relatively little about their preferences. As befits pure meat-eaters though, they seem to have a limited ability to detect sweetness, which possibly links with our cats' inability to digest sugars. This is one reason why milk, which contains it own sugar, lactose, gives many cats diarrhoea. The taste buds that are found on the back, sides and tip of your cat's tongue do allow him to taste salt, bitter and sour flavours.

Smell

All cats rely on odour for sending and receiving information, and your cat has highly developed scent-detection abilities. A cat's nose is lined with a membrane that is twice as extensive as ours, folded so that it contains millions of specialized odour-detecting cells.

However, cats have an additional ability to taste rather than smell substances they come into contact with physically, using what is called the vomeronasal organ (Jacobson's organ). This pair of pouch-like organs is situated in the roof of your cat's mouth and has an opening just behind his small front teeth, the incisors. It is only used intermittently, and you may see your pet doing the so-called Flehmen response, which is a sort of grimace, when he pulls back his upper lip, with his mouth open to help concentrate the odorous material. This is a behaviour particularly associated with courtship and mating, but neutered cats also exhibit the Flehmen response.

Above: *Although little is known about cats' sense of taste, we do know that their tastebuds allow them to taste salt, bitter and sour flavours.*

Left: *Cats' eyes, so well adapted to hunting, are not only beautiful but also reflect their emotions.*

BINOCULAR VISION
Both people and cats have binocular vision, but anatomical differences mean that compared to us they have a somewhat wider visual field, so our cats can see more to each side than we can. However, the amount of binocular overlap (the area to the front where the images from each eye converge, helping with judging distance and depth) is much the same in our two species.

Above: Cats naturally use 3D space, which means they often prefer to be high up. To help our pets de-stress, we can replicate this inside our homes by providing elevated resting and hiding places.

Right: The female cat is left alone to raise offspring, teaching them survival skills until they leave her after gaining sexual maturity.

Survival and territory

In the wild, cats evolved to be active at dawn and dusk, when their prey animals are out. They seek somewhere to shelter through the heat of the day so that they can conserve their reserves, only becoming energized again when temperatures cool and the animals they hunt are to be found. This crepuscular (twilight) behaviour persists even in domesticated pets, which can be a problem for sleepy owners.

Keeping out of danger

The world can be hazardous for an animal as small as the cat, and it was vital that the earliest cats developed strategies to reduce the risk of injury or the chances of being the prey of another animal. Hiding and climbing are, therefore, important features of the cat's behavioural repertoire. Their skeletons have become adapted for graceful acrobatics, and they have claws that can effectively grasp trunks and bark (as well as prey), enabling them to shin up trees and navigate flimsy branches, using their outstretched tails to counterbalance their weight. The ability to crouch silently in the smallest crevice until danger has passed would have made the difference between life and death in your cat's ancestral home.

Passing on genes

In the natural world surviving as a species is vitally important. Male and female cats lead separate lives, except during the breeding season, when a combination of scent and vocal communication helps them come together briefly to mate, after which the male takes no further part in the process. Raising the offspring is entirely a task for the mother. It's also her responsibility to teach her offspring all the skills they will need to become successful hunters and to survive and thrive after they disperse at sexual maturity. If times are good and living is relatively easy, they may linger a little longer, but in this harsh environment the lone state tends to rule.

Territory and survival

In the world in which your cat's free-living ancestor had to make a living and successfully reproduce so that both individual and species genes could endure, resources (food and shelter) were crucially important, but so too was the area that contains them. The richer the pickings, the smaller the territory required to sustain a single cat and, for a female cat, her offspring. Less energy is expended and fewer risks have to be taken in defending a small area against competitors. When prey is scarce or when refuges from weather and predators are hard to find, however, a larger area is required to survive.

Territoriality, therefore, is a feature of feline society, and it persists even in the pets that share our homes (see also pages 46–51). Of course, when doting humans provide the important resources of food and shelter the motivation of individual cats to defend their range varies considerably. You may find that your cat quickly establishes his 'patch' and defends it with vigour. It's equally possible that he will adopt a more relaxed attitude and be happy to share with neighbouring felines. It all depends on his lineage, early upbringing and individual personality. One thing is certain, however: animals, including our cats, have no sense whatsoever of 'fair play'. When it comes to something they really, really want, they want it now – all of it. This can be upsetting for owners but it is wrong to try and impose our value systems on our pets.

Communication

Territoriality is not without its problems. Active defence is a risky business, and any cat that mounts an attack may be injured, and distracted animals are more at risk than those that are alert to possible hazards. Even small wounds inflicted by a competitor can reduce a cat's ability to hunt, and infection from fight injuries may quickly become life threatening.

Scent helps reduce risk

Cats have developed strategies to advertise their 'ownership' of territory and to minimize the need for defensive aggression. Principally, they use scent marking, such as bunting and urine spraying, to stake their claims. The closer cats are to each other, the bigger the risk that things will get physical, so odour is widely used in feline society (see also page 17). It can convey significant information without the need for actual contact between the signaller and 'receiver'. There is the added advantage that even though it gradually fades, it's still there sending out the message some while after the resident has moved on.

Specially adapted skin glands around the mouth, head, feet, flanks and tail produce the scents that cats use to anoint various objects in their environment. They also deposit urine, and sometimes faeces, for the same purpose. The particular scenting behaviour varies according to prevailing circumstances and the information they want to convey. In addition to laying claim to territory, cats use odour to advertise their availability as mates and to indicate their health and emotional status.

Nearer home the behaviour can reassure them that their patch is well labelled as theirs. In a group of domesticated cats the marking can identify individuals and identify them as members of a family or community. Developed in the wild for a very specific purpose, scent marking is

another good example of an aspect of behaviour that persists in our pets today. Unfortunately, it's another one that often puts cats at odds with their owners.

Close up and personal

The fact that cats rely so much on scent doesn't mean that they don't communicate using body language, facial expression or their voices. Obviously, they can tell much more about each other if they risk getting closer and combine scent with visual signals, but they are, in fact, much more effective close-quarter communicators than many people realize. Their subtlety is in such sharp contrast to our other main animal companion, the dog, that it is all too easily overlooked or misunderstood.

As you will probably have noticed, your cat uses his facial expressions and ear and whisker positions to good effect and can signal his intentions and how he feels quite clearly with his eyes. His body language is also a good indicator of his emotional state, helping to signal what he is likely to do next. All cats use a range of postures and tail positions, and bluffing is also a significant part of the feline behavioural repertoire. If you own a cat it's well worth becoming familiar with his ability to mislead. Many an apparent feline 'underdog' has effectively seen off a potential rival or territorial intruder by raising his tail to its fullest height, fluffing himself up, pricking up his ears, staring hard at the other cat and simply

pretending to be much bigger and stronger than he really is.
If you watch your cat closely you will probably soon get
used to judging his mood and quickly understand how he
feels about a certain visitor, for example, or how he will
react when he sees your neighbour's cat invading his territory,
even if he's an indoor cat and observing through the window.

Above: *Don't mistake an aroused cat's
prelude to attack with the relaxed pose of
the cat above or you could be badly hurt.*

Left: *A cat's fur will fluff up when faced
with an unwanted intruder in the garden
in an attempt to make himself look as big
as possible.*

SUBMISSION
Many people have been hurt because they didn't
understand that cats just don't have submission
in their repertoire. When they roll over on their
backs it's not that they are giving up. It's so that
they can even more efficiently use all five of their
weapons: fours sets of claws and one very effective
set of teeth.

Chats between cats

If you live with a cat that 'talks' you may wonder if vocal communication is used in the wild. Any creature that is as vulnerable as our cats' original ancestors were is unlikely to survive long by drawing attention to himself, so cats lack the lion's ability to roar. Vocal interaction is really limited only to kittenhood, mating and the occasional close encounter.

Mother and offspring

When the queen returns to the nest with food she locates her offspring by chirruping. While they can solicit her help through distress calls, and as they grow and explore more widely they find her and each other using sound. Both mother and kittens purr when they are quiet and contented, and the defensive hiss is learned at a very early age.

When they are mature and living independently, both males and females locate potential mates using sound as well as scent, and vocal messages are employed to intimidate territorial intruders.

Throughout the course of history closer association both with people and others of their own kind, has cultivated the vocal repertoire of the domesticated cat, and your cat has the potential to use a range of sounds. Some, such as the purr or the greeting trill or chirrup you may hear, are made with the mouth closed. For other sounds, however, he will open then gradually close his mouth. The miaow is made this way, although obviously some pets are more vocal than others. If your cat is aroused by fear or is defending his territory, the intensity of his growl, snarl, hiss, spit or yowl – all sounds made with a fixed-mouth position – may take you by surprise.

Above: *Careful observation and a knowledge of feline subtlety helps us to understand our cats' emotional states and can often modify our preconceptions.*

Left: *This cat is defending his territory using a fixed-mouth position. This howl or spit differs from a usual 'miaow' which is made by the cat as he gradually closes his mouth.*

Defusing tension

Tensions can run high in any community, especially in the face of scarcity or outside threat, and when they get together cats are no different in this respect. We also know that one of their instincts is to avoid active conflict and its risks. So, it stands to reason that where cats come into contact with each other or live together, as they do now that they are domesticated, they need a means not only of communicating with each other but also of resolving conflict when things get tense.

For a long time it was believed that cats do not really communicate very well at all, partly at least because, as we've seen, feline communication systems lack the overt gestures we're so familiar with in our dogs (see page 20). Recently, however, it's become increasingly clear that cats do communicate, although their subtlety still frequently catches us out. We now understand that cats use their body language, together with facial expression, scent rubbing and grooming, to relieve tension after close contact and to make themselves, and others, feel better after a spat.

The most significant factor, however, is that cats do not have the overt appeasement gestures that dogs do. Cats use low-key measures to restore harmony in a less obvious manner. For example, you might notice that your cat blinks or turns his head if you stare at him for some minutes. In feline terms you are challenging him. He, in his turn, is indicating that he is not a threat to you because he will not retaliate. Alternatively, you might see him in the garden confronted by a neighbouring cat. Your cat might be simply sitting, with his gaze averted, or very slowly turning and slinking away, after making himself as small as he can.

Purring is a form of communication seen throughout the cat family. It's not restricted to the small or domesticated cats, although interactions with people may enhance the willingness of our pets to purr frequently and loudly. Perhaps astonishingly, we're still unclear about the exact mechanism that generates the purr, although a range of ideas has been suggested.

The purring enigma

HOW CATS PURR

No one seems to know exactly how cats make the sound that we call purring. The process appears to be quite complicated and to involve more than just a build-up of pressure in the glottis (voice box) that separates the vocal folds when it is released. The cardio-vascular system probably has some significance in the process too, but no one is certain. It is known that it occurs during both inhalation and exhalation, which makes it seem almost continuous, although there is a slight pause between the respiratory phases. The inhalation component of the purr is often longer, louder and lower pitched than the exhalation part, but individual cats vary.

WHY DO CATS PURR?

Just as no one is really certain *how* cats purr, no one is entirely sure *why* cats purr. It is known that purring is generally associated with pleasure and contentment and that kittens are able to make this sound almost from birth. Both mother and offspring purr when she is suckling her kittens, and it seems likely that their vocalization, combined with the paw paddling the kittens also do, helps to stimulate the mother's milk to flow. For humans, a cat's purr tends to have a calming or relaxing effect on our senses.

When they become more active, the kittens' purring provides a useful means by which the family group can locate each other, keep together and provide communal reassurance without drawing attention to the nest. It has been suggested that this type of purring functions rather like a human smile to help establish the important relationship between cats, especially as it is also heard during courtship. However, this may simply be a case of scientists becoming uncharacteristically anthropomorphic.

FOOD FIRST

During the first few weeks of a kitten's life purring is part of the greeting vocalization when the queen returns to the nest, and it is probably a reliable signal to the other kittens that food is available. This aspect tends to continue into adulthood with our cats, which approach us purring and rubbing round our legs when we are heading towards the cupboard where their food is kept.

In fact, once they're grown up, the purr features in a range of social situations that involve contact with other familiar cats or people with whom cats feel comfortable, and this has led to the suggestion that it is a hangover from kittenhood and is used as a care-

HEALING THROUGH PURRING

It has been suggested that the frequency of the purr – about 25 Hz or cycles per second, irrespective of sex, age, size or weight – may have healing properties. The increasing use of intrasound (from 20 to 20,000 Hz) as opposed to ultrasound (above 20,000 Hz) therapy in human medicine, especially in orthopaedics, to promote blood flow and healing, may mean that this is not as farfetched as it seems.

soliciting vocalization – that is, it's used to get our attention. In these circumstances, behaviour such as rolling or rubbing on the ground, on inanimate objects or their owners may serve the same purpose – the cat is trying to get something it wants.

Surprisingly and sadly, however, cats also purr when they are *in extremis* – if they are very frightened, seriously ill or badly injured. The possibilities are that in such difficult circumstances they are trying to reassure themselves – a self-appeasing gesture that helps to calm them down by reducing stress and, if people are around, sociable well-domesticated individuals may be trying to solicit assistance.

Undoubtedly, however, the reality is that the whole range of purposes for which the purr developed is yet to be discovered and this remains an area of research for the future.

Left: Kittens are able to purr from birth and it is likely that this, along with paw paddling, helps to stimulate milk flow.

Below: Cats charming habits often shape their owners' behaviour, demonstrating the opportunism that underpins their species' evolutionary success.

Above: If they're raised appropriately together, dogs and cats often bond firmly to each other but we should never forget that their species behaviour is different.

Right: Cats group together in colonies only if they have discovered a reliable source of food in a single place, such as in the Colosseum in Rome.

The social cat

Domestication brought to cats the benefits of reliable food and shelter, and this has inevitably changed, albeit only gradually, the nature of our cats. The previously asocial animal began to be a little tolerant of closer contact with people and even its own kind. When we look at our cats, however, it's important to remember that the established behaviours of their solitary forebears are lurking just beneath the surface.

Changing patterns

Although we have brought cats into our homes as rodent controllers and companions, with the exception of the pedigree breeds, the cat as a species has experienced relatively little human interference with its breeding. This contrasts sharply with the dog, where selective breeding over centuries has resulted in a range of widely differing sizes, appearances and behavioural traits, which were specifically developed to fill a number of different roles in human lives – hunting, guarding, shepherding sheep and so on.

It's also important to bear in mind that the more recently socialized cat is not the same sort of social animal as the dog. Those people who don't realize that there is this significant difference between our two principal pet species will always struggle to understand their cats.

Living like a dog brings benefits

Dogs are pack animals. Their distant ancestor, the wolf, developed different survival strategies from the solitary hunting feline from which your cat evolved. The really important difference is that wolves don't just live in groups – something that cats will do under certain circumstances – but they hunt as a team, too. This has the benefit that bigger prey animals can be caught. Larger meals reduce the need for continuous hunting, which is the pattern that cats, subsisting on much smaller, less nutritious meals, must adopt.

Moreover, cooperative enterprise provides a support system for raising offspring and for less robust individuals, which may have become weakened through age or injury. However, it also means that an understanding has to develop about how the prey's carcass will be divided up, or the animals will risk injury, waste energy and make themselves vulnerable to competitors – and to the occasional larger predator, such as bears – if they spent time squabbling over a kill.

The typical canine hierarchy with which many of us are familiar (and which we may also misunderstand) developed as a sort of basis for 'orderly queuing' at the dinner table. This is established and maintained through everything the animals do at other times, including socializing, grooming and communal nursing.

Cats are not small dogs

The crucial difference between canine and feline group living is that cats always maintain their independence when it comes to obtaining food. If they are entirely dependent on their own efforts to eat they will hunt alone and do not usually share kills, except with their kittens. Cats may congregate around the food source if humans provide some or all of the food, but they do so simply because the food is often only found in a single place. In other words, cats share only because they have to.

Cats do not have a hierarchy. The only 'queuing' that occurs is that the boldest or most desperate come first, with the most timid and weakest getting the leftovers. If the food supply is reliable, because it is provided say by one dedicated person or even a restaurant's rubbish bins, a fairly stable group of cats may develop and live in the same area. There are places where such colonies have become well established – for example, the cats of the Colosseum in Rome. If, on the other hand, the food supply is intermittent and unreliable, it's unlikely that many cats will spend much time in a particular location. They will be individually scavenging or hunting over a wider area in search of enough food to survive. This is another example of how resources, such as food, rather than just instincts, will dictate how cats, wild and domesticated, behave.

Can cats live together?

The answer to the question of whether cats can live together is a qualified 'yes'. There is still much to discover, but we've learned a lot in recent years from studying the lifestyles and relationship dynamics of 'un-owned' cats in a range of locations. Scientists are not in complete agreement about the significance of some of the evidence that has been uncovered, but our understanding of the 'natural behaviour' of our cats has increased enormously.

The benefits for cats of group living

Domestic cats are classified in three groups:

- Feral, which are domestic cats that are 'born in the wild'; unless these animals are taken into human care at a few weeks of age they are unlikely to become sociable with people.
- Semi-feral, which are pets that have reverted to an un-owned lifestyle or cats that are only partly dependent on humans, such as farm cats, which are kept to control vermin but also provided with some additional food.
- Pets, which are cats whose every need is met by a human.

Above: *Studying free-living cats has significantly increased our understanding of the pets that share our homes.*

Right: *Natural cat colonies are based around a matriachy where the females raise the young, caring for kittens of other mothers as well as their own.*

Scientific studies of cats in the first two groups have been informative, and the nearest we can get to looking at domestic cats living in natural conditions is where, largely free of human interference, they congregate in a location that offers sufficient shelter and reliably 'rich pickings' in terms of food. Studies have been undertaken in a range of different locations, such as dockyards, farms and institutions like hospitals, all places where colonies of cats are tolerated though not really cared for.

Where food is plentiful cats will form quite large groups, which are based around a matriarchy. Females collectively raise the young, defending, suckling and caring for the kittens of other mothers as well as their own. This makes sense because they are related to each other, and the extended family's survival depends on this cooperative effort.

When conditions are good, the core group will tolerate other cats hanging around the colony. However, these cats are never fully included, and they have a much tougher time getting enough to eat and access to the most desirable nesting places. If times get harder they are even ejected. As a result, the breeding rate of the 'outsiders' is lower than that of members of the main group, and the outsiders' kittens have poorer chances of survival than those of the matriarchy.

Males are generally loosely attached to a number of female groups and roam among them, so their territories are larger than those of the mothers of their offspring. Competition among males for mating rights can be fierce, although the males take little part in raising the young once they are born. This pattern is quite different from that in the increasingly popular multi-cat household, where cats cannot control membership of their colony. In our homes cat groups are based on the whim of their owners, and significant numbers of behavioural problems develop because of a failure to recognize this one significant fact: cats need to feel in control of their lives.

Different circumstances, different behaviour

Another issue that has been studied – and one that is important for those of us who own cats – is the behaviour that cats exhibit when different amounts of food are available. In difficult circumstances where food is scarce cats tend to live alone, much as their ancestors did. Seeking shelter where they can, they range over considerable distances in search of prey or other sources of sustenance. Defence of their territory against competitors is fierce, because keeping it means the difference between life and death. Because the terrain they inhabit does not provide enough to sustain a group of cats, solitary mothers raise their offspring alone, but as soon as the youngsters reach sexual maturity they disperse.

This pattern of competition for important resources can be seen in our cats even after a number of generations. If your cat came originally from a family that had to survive by their own wits, he may find it more difficult to share his home, food, toys and your attention than a cat whose family traditionally had an easier time of it.

Do cats have friends?

Inevitably, some cats – like some people – seem to be more sociable than others. You may notice that your cat has some feline friends he regularly seeks out, whereas he is completely indifferent, even hostile, to other cats. Recent studies of un-owned cats have revealed that this characteristic is also seen in free-living cats.

THE STORY SO FAR

It's becoming increasingly common to find colonies of cats in which some members have been cared for at some stage in their lives, then been abandoned or lost and have then reverted 'to the wild'. Others, although 'born free', have often been taken into 'trap, neuter and release' schemes. Therefore, because many of these un-owned cats are unable to breed, the groups frequently consist of individuals that have come together as neutered adults, rather than being born and raised as a family community. If essential resources are provided, these cats often form stable groups that can live together for years, which makes their circumstances much more like the conditions that exist in our own homes when there is more than one pet cat.

Studies of these colonies have been teaching us quite a lot, both about the dynamics of multi-cat households and also the lives of singleton pets that have access to outdoors in urban environments, where the local feline population is high. Forcing cats to exist in close proximity to each other evidently has implications for their welfare, so the more we can understand about feline relationships the better.

As with so much of our cats' behaviour, we still have much to learn, but studies of this sort are certainly helping us to increase our knowledge of what our cats do and, most importantly, to begin to understand why they do what they do.

FELINE FRIENDS

A cat's individual temperament and early experiences obviously play some part in his reaction when he meets another cat or cats – just as they do with us – but we now know that in any more or less stable feline group, what scientists call 'affiliations' (and what we might call feline friendships) will develop – that is, one, two or occasionally three individuals will be frequently observed sitting in close proximity to each other. Scientists refer to the cats in these affiliations as 'preferred associates'.

One of the problems facing the researchers is that it can be difficult to be certain that these relationships are based on more than the fact that cats congregate in and around the area where food is dispensed. Interestingly, however, it has been found that preferred associates are seen close to each other at different times of day in various locations, thus indicating that they really are choosing to spend time

in each other's company and are not just forced to do so out of necessity.

Once such a group of preferred associates has become established and the cats have become familiar with each other, they are seen indulging in the sort of greeting and bonding behaviours that have been observed between family members in colonies of related felines.

FELINE BONDING BEHAVIOUR
Cats generally exhibit four main types of bonding behaviour:

• Allogrooming
• Allorubbing
• Nose touching
• Play

Allogrooming describes one cat licking another, usually around the head and neck, and it is usually seen when cats are resting together. It is reciprocal in nature, and as well as maintaining bonds between them, it seems to be used to re-establish harmony after tense encounters between cats.

Allorubbing describes two cats pushing against each other with their heads, bodies and tails. This behaviour is often more one-sided than allogrooming, with a weaker cat directing its attentions towards an older, more confident or established cat. This tactile form of communication has the advantage of mixing individual scents to form a group or community odour.

Nose touching is a social greeting behaviour that is seen mostly between preferred associates.

Play is less commonly seen in adult cats than in youngsters, but occasionally it is observed among cats in an affiliation.

Above: Allogrooming and allorubbing are two examples of bonding behaviour that cats display.

Left: Just like humans, cats' body language and behaviour generally indicate how comfortable individuals are when in close contact with each other.

How do cats view us?

Whether they have just one or several feline companions, most owners will, at one time or another, wonder how their cats feel about them. Despite making every effort to bond with their cat, an owner can never be certain if they're regarded as a potential threat or with disdain because they're big and clumsy. Do cats think of us as satisfactory companions or just rather feeble hunters to whom they must bring prey?

Tolerance or affection?

Your cat's relationship with you and your human companions – the rest of your family – appears to be as complex, variable and subtle as your cat's relationships with other cats.

Just like us, cats genuinely seem to have individual styles of interaction with others, including people. A range of factors will affect any cat's willingness – and even his ability – to interact with people generally and his owners in particular. Temperament and upbringing have a significant influence on feline sociability towards humans, with some cats boldly approaching complete strangers, whereas others are shy and timid, even with people they know well.

The whole topic of the relationships between cats and owners, especially in terms of the animals' perception of that relationship, has not been the subject of much scrutiny, so our views are largely based on conjecture. What we can be certain of, however, is that many pets behave towards their owners in much the same was as their free-living cousins behave towards other cats in their family group. They seem to seek us out, 'bunt' us with their heads (see page 52), rub around our legs and twine their tails around us. Whether we intend to or not, we exchange scents in this process, thus contributing to a reassuring colony or community odour. It's quite possible that the cats are simply responding to us as they do to other large and potentially scary objects in the environment – making us less threatening by marking us as theirs and nothing more.

However, when we've been apart our cats do tend to greet us vocally and with their tails straight up in a signal of confidence, which is something they do with other cats to which they are bonded. This behaviour makes the relationship between us seem more intimate than simple marking behaviour would suggest.

Are we surrogate 'parents'?

In turn, we usually talk to our cats and often stroke them – a gesture that has no direct feline equivalent, but one that could be interpreted as our version of allorubbing or even allogrooming (see page 31). So, we do seem to serve as part of a feline group for some sociably disposed pets. Other cats, of course, are more reserved, but exactly how any of them view us is a different matter.

We also tend by the process of neutering to change our cats' reproductive state, so behaviourally they retain some juvenile or adolescent characteristics. Consequently, we allow our pets all the pleasures of kittenhood without the responsibilities that come with growing up. This gives credibility to the theory that because of our size and our role in supplying their essential resources, cats tend to view us as adult members of their community. Their habit of greeting us and soliciting our attention with vocalizations, including purring, as they do to their mothers, also ties in with this way of thinking. We, of course, reciprocate when we nurture them. It has even been suggested that cats like sitting on our laps because the warmth and 'hollow' thus provided is reminiscent of the curve formed by the nursing queen's body, into which her kittens snuggle for food and comfort.

Are cats the real providers?

A contrary view to those who think that cats regard their owners as some kind of large mother, is the one that suggests that some cats return to their homes with prey because they view us as being incapable of hunting effectively. Therefore, the argument goes, the cat is offering us opportunities to practise our hunting skills. It could, of course, simply be the case that your cat brings prey back to his core area but then doesn't quite know how to deal with it, for reasons we'll examine later (see pages 40–1).

In addition, we spend time with our cats and play with them and, especially if they are kept indoors, provide most of their opportunities for interaction and stimulation. This is something that is important with many bright, reactive and sociable individuals for whom human companionship does seem to be a necessary and enjoyed 'resource'. It's quite possible, therefore, that your cat simply views you as something that's not threatening and that is, on the whole, advantageous to have around.

We shape each other's behaviour

Until we can really get inside the feline head and read our cats' every thought, the discussion will go on. For many of us, however, our cats, whether we have a singleton or multi-cat group, are part of the family. We enjoy providing for them and nurturing them, in effect acting as their mother, aunts and cousins would during their kittenhood in a family group.

We also shape their behaviour by what is known as 'conditioning' their habits. For instance, many of us have feeding signals – uttering phrases such as 'Here kitty, kitty' in higher than normal voices (often to the amusement of our neighbours no doubt) to tell them to come to the kitchen.

Our cats, of course, have the same effect on us. Many owners, for example, have difficulty in writing letters, using their computers or approaching the refrigerator without 'help' from a favoured feline friend. In fact, many pets have irritating but endearing habits that bind us more firmly to them.

Left: Some feline habits, such as returning home with prey, are less endearing than others, but it's always interesting to search for the motivation underlying the behaviour.

Interestingly, we do know that cat-initiated interactions between pets and owners last longer and are more intense than when people make the initial overtures. Understanding this can be useful when you are trying to repair strained relationships between cats and owners or when you are establishing new bonds with your own or someone else's cat. Imposing attention is quite the wrong thing to do. Allowing a cat to make the first approach, then being sure that you reciprocate, perhaps just using your voice at first, no matter how inconvenient it may be, is the quickest and most trouble-free approach to building good cat–human relationships.

Doing the best for your cat

The way each individual pet regards his owner may differ from cat to cat, and perhaps what matters most is that you should make the utmost effort to understand your cat's physical and psychological needs and then to provide him with the best quality of life you can. To do this, you need to know:

- How your cat behaves.
- How you should read his signals and body language.
- How genetics and 'personality' influence his behaviour.
- What happened in your cat's early life that might affect him as an adult.
- How your lifestyle can stress your cat or keep him calm.
- How your cat will react in health and sickness.
- How your cat is likely to be affected by everyday and by 'special' events.

Last but not least, you have to know what problems can arise with your cat's behaviour if you get things wrong or if he fails to cope well with the world in which he finds himself. The more we learn, the better we will know the cat, or cats, we live with and love, and the better owners we will become.

NORMAL BEHAVIOUR

It is not unreasonable to ask if our pets have changed during the cat's long journey from savannah to human home and hearth. The simple answer is that, despite the easier living many cats now enjoy, their behaviour hasn't altered as much as you might think. No doubt the seed of all your pet's fascinating and entertaining behaviour today lies in what his ancestors needed to do to survive and thrive in the various environments in which they found themselves. As we look at the different aspects of your cat's behaviour you will no doubt enjoy comparing what he does now to the purpose for which each particular trait originally developed.

Predatory behaviour

It's a source of puzzlement to many people that a well-fed cat will continue to hunt. Obviously, some cats are more motivated than others, and some are remarkably effective, while there are a few cats that are completely clueless. Before we condemn the successful hunters out of hand, however, it's worth looking at just why it happens.

Hunting

That a skilled hunter will not be averse to going straight out from his satisfying dinner into the dusk to wreck havoc among the local rodent population is certainly unsettling. Even more distressing for some owners is the cat's tendency to bring 'prizes' back to base, which can be particularly unpleasant when, next morning, you step on the remains that have been left in the hall or on the landing.

When we think about it, however, it makes sense that a cat's hunting and feeding behaviours are controlled by different parts of the brain. It's unlikely that any animal which depended on catching his own meals would survive for very long if he waited until hunger pangs urged him off on a foraging trip. If prey were scare, he might well be too weak to acquire a meal when he needed one, which would have devastating long-term consequences for him and possibly his species. Even when the living is easy and effortless – thanks to the tireless devotion of

willing humans – predatory animals will hunt in some form or other. So you may see your cat go through the motions several times a day, even if he never actually catches anything apart from his toys or the shoelace you inadvertently dangle before him.

Many of us worry about the effect of the rising domestic cat population on birds that are already struggling with the consequences of climate change and habitat loss. In some areas of Australia, for example, laws now restrict the free roaming of cats in an attempt to protect local native species. This is evidently a special case, because as many owners can testify, the effectiveness of their cats' predatory prowess is debatable. Even though fledglings are especially vulnerable during breeding seasons, studies have shown that rodents are the preferred prey of most cats. Sometimes owners can help by making sure their cats have lots of interesting and stimulating activities to occupy their time and by providing plentiful appropriate artificial outlets for their predatory instincts (see pages 114–5 and 126–7).

The hunting or predatory sequence

The cat's established hunting sequence will consist of:

- Watching
- Stalking
- Chasing
- Pouncing
- Killing

Crouched down in the grass or behind a bush, his toes tucked in, your cat may appear to be doing nothing. The chances are, however, that all his senses are tuned for any rustle, vibration or slight movement that indicates that prey is nearby. If it's close, he could launch straight into a pounce, first raising his rear end and wiggling his bottom in preparation for lift-off. Or you may see him stalking, keeping low, moving very slowly and purposefully with his eyes fixed on a particular spot, before sprinting after the prey, then leaping up in the air in a graceful arc to land on the hapless mouse he's had his eye on. Out come his normally sheathed claws to grasp and prevent

Left: *Cats go through the motions of hunting during the day, even if they are not catching prey. Instead they will practise on toys or catching shoelaces.*

Above: *Once trapped, prey is located more by vibration and smell than sight, which is better adapted to perceiving fast moving objects some distance away.*

its escape. Then, if he's an effective hunter or if he's hungry, he may dispatch the animal quite quickly with an effective bite to its neck that severs the spinal column.

Playing with prey

Sadly, another aspect of behaviour that causes much human distress is the cat's habit of apparently getting pleasure out of 'torturing' any creature he gets hold of. However, to view this behaviour in relation to prey in terms of entertainment and enjoyment is actually to miss the point.

Cats aren't any more cruel than nature, 'red in tooth and claw', is. What they do is dictated by necessity and the need to make their lives as risk free as possible. Weakening a potential meal before getting it really close to his face makes sense.

A sharp beak can blind a cat, and even a small wound inflicted by the teeth of a rodent could become infected, leading to weakening or life-threatening infections, a risk that's best avoided. Making the prey move by poking and paw patting until it becomes disorientated and loses its strength is

a useful way to achieve just that. The vigour of the creature's avoiding action will also be a useful way in which the cat can assess the risk involved in this particular situation and if it's a risk worth taking or not.

Bringing back the booty

The cat's motives for this rather unappealing trait are still being debated. A practical purpose could be that once it is out of its normal habitat, any creature becomes disorientated and less able to escape. In addition, enjoying a potential meal in a safe environment certainly has merit. Then there's the theory (see page 35) that a cat that returns with a kill believes he needs to teach his owner to hunt or plans to share the opportunity to practise their predatory skills with other cats if they share their home.

Whatever its purpose, the action often leads to conflict between owners and pets. It's a particular concern when a cat that is unskilled at effectively stringing together the whole hunting sequence or delivering the crucial killing bite, as so many domesticated cats are, puts down the creature he's carried home in his mouth. If it's not sufficiently stunned or

weakened, it may scurry away under furniture or floorboards. At that stage it's not unusual for the would-be killer to lose interest, although some cats spend the next few days staring patiently at the exact spot where the quarry disappeared, apparently unaware of all the potential avenues of escape open to it.

Practice makes perfect

Undoubtedly many cats never become skilled at combining the different steps of the predatory sequence. Why would they need to do so if they've never had to fend for themselves? How would they know how to do so if their mothers were equally ineffective and lacked the skills to teach them the basics? This explains why some pets can catch things but then seem unsure what to do next. Deprived of the need to make a living in the big, wide world, many of our cats expend energy on 'prey' items that have little in the way of calorific content – butterflies, moths and flies, for example. These might be a source of 'famine food' for felines in the wild, but unless a self-supporting cat can acquire many more nutritious meals, it is pretty well doomed to failure.

Another aspect of the cat's status as a pet that is relevant to this behaviour is the fact that unless our cats unfortunately fall on hard times, through abandonment or accidental loss, they never really have to grow up, in the sense of

Above: Hunting, like all our cats' other skills, is something that must be learned and watching a youngster's ineffective practice attempts is often an amusing occupation.

Left: Cats will 'play' with their prey to stun it before bringing it to their mouths to avoid any injuries they may receive from beaks, teeth or claws.

providing for themselves. We neuter (de-sex) them (see pages 98–99), which prevents them from reaching sexual maturity, with all that entails, and we nurture them. Of course, this doesn't apply to every domestic cat. Some are remarkably keen and effective predators, seemingly at the top of their game, sometimes for years on end, but in the main pet cats are likely to engage in hunting only because they stumble across opportunities. On the whole, for most cats playing with artificial prey items suffices just as well.

Eating

When cats were lone hunters, dependant on their own efforts for satisfying their hunger, they had to be fit and well so that they could catch and kill their prey as quickly and safely as possible. As a result, they have skulls that have evolved to make this possible – as long, of course, as they have the necessary skills to find a meal in the first place.

The essential anatomy

A cat's face is relatively shortened, which lends strength to the muscles and jaws, while he has fewer teeth than most other carnivores. All the teeth, except the tiny front incisors, which are important for grooming, are robust and adapted for meat eating, being capable of tearing and shearing. You'll see the differences displayed when your cat yawns, but you might also notice that he's not so good at chewing, and the dental structure explains why cats so often appear to gulp when they are eating or trying to rid themselves of a mouthful of hair during their cleaning routines. It can also lead to some of them getting grass 'stuck in their gullets'.

Feeding patterns

We tend to feed our cats once or twice a day, often a timetable that's dictated by tradition or, more often, by our own convenience. Combined with the more sedentary lifestyle adopted by our generally pampered cats, this may well be contributing to the current 'epidemic' of feline obesity (see also pages 124–5). Such a pattern seems to rob some cats of the ability to regulate the amounts they consume, so they end up eating for a potential famine, as it were, just because the food's there, rather than snacking and coming back later for some more.

In addition, of course, many owners express their affection through food, providing far too many calories. This can be a particular problem with commercially prepared dry formulations, because the recommended amount for the weight, size and age of a pet invariably seems so parsimonious that people cannot bring themselves to offer their favourite friend so little. Such kindness is misguided, but by making feeding time fun and trying to simulate the natural pattern of 10–12, possibly up to 16, mouse-sized portions a day, everyone will benefit.

Fussy eaters

Despite being opportunistic feeders, cats have a reputation for being finicky pets to cater for. We still have a great deal to learn about feline food selection, something that causes many owners much frustration. It makes sense for animals that encounter many hazards in their natural environment to be

Left: The way we feed our pet cats is currently the subject of much debate in the face of the growing feline obesity 'epidemic'.

Right: Eating non-toxic plants and grass can be good for a cat's digestive system. Keep an eye out if he keeps coughing afterwards in case a trip to the vet is needed.

fastidious about what they will and won't eat, especially as cats are not particularly well equipped to deal with toxins. So pets tend to avoid foods that are completely novel to them – it's a characteristic called neophobia.

On the other hand, some cats do get bored with the same old thing and will try new foods as long as they are in a familiar form, whether canned or dry composition. They often quickly return to the original brand of food – usually, of course, when you've just stocked up on the new one.

It's unclear how much a cat's food preferences are inherited and how much they are learned from early experiences, but what does seem certain is that palatability involves appearance, taste, smell, texture and temperature, with taste being the most important. This is why it's important to tempt ailing cats or elderly pets with a compromised sense of smell by warming their food to make it more aromatic and nearer body temperature.

EATING GRASS

Eating non-toxic plants provides roughage to keep the cat's digestive tract healthy, but sometimes long blades of some types of grass curl up round the palate (roof of the mouth) and travel down the nose. Don't worry if your cat spends time outdoors and enjoys chewing grass – that's quite normal – but if he coughs afterwards for more than a short time quickly take him to your veterinarian for a check-up.

Growing cat-friendly grasses in your garden or in pots inside for indoor cats is a good idea.

Drinking

A cat's drinking habits often puzzle and concern his owners. It can also be a cause of some amusement as a cat indulges in antics like drinking the shower water as it drains down the plughole or balancing precariously on the edge of a full tub to investigate the top of the bath water.

CATS NEED WATER

In recent decades the number of owners feeding their cats dry foods has significantly increased. However, the hygiene and convenience advantages of such formulations go hand in hand with some significant medical implications and as a result the issue of cats drinking is receiving a lot of attention.

In the natural environment free-living cats get most, if not all, of their fluid requirements from their food. Owners sometimes say that they provide fresh water, but their cats completely ignore it, day after day, year after year. No one should ever stop supplying the water if this happens, but simply putting a dish down by your cat's food bowl, even when the water is replaced every day, may not be enough to encourage your cat to drink.

THE REAL STORY

In the wild cats that do seek out a water hole or puddle to drink from do not eat at the same place. They hunt at different times and in different locations. So from your cat's point of view the practice of putting his water and food bowls next to each other doesn't make much sense.

Cats like to be able to see the meniscus (the surface) at the top of the water to help them judge their distance from it – it puts them off if they can't – so a small static bowlful of liquid often doesn't achieve much in this respect.

Some cats will be put off drinking if their whiskers touch the sides of the dish, and others don't like the unnatural taste of highly processed tapwater. Still other cats require the freshly oxygenated stream provided by a constantly running tap, which also moves so they can see it clearly.

The secret is to avoid making assumptions about your cat's preferences, or taking the easy option.

MONITORING INTAKE

Make sure that you monitor your cat's normal patterns and find out whether he drinks a lot because he has dry food or virtually nothing because you give him a largely wet (canned) diet. Then you'll be aware of any increased thirst that might indicate that something is not right and you might need to consult your vet.

INCREASING INTAKE

There are several ways of encouraging your cat to increase his fluid intake, and you should experiment a little to see what works best for him.

- Try a range of different containers: tall and deep, wide and flat, an outsized drinking glass or an old-fashioned soup plate, for instance.
- Position the containers at various locations around your home.
- Leave a tap dripping.
- Buy a commercial pet fountain that produces a continuous stream of recycled water; these are especially useful with blind or partially-sighted cats that can locate their water from

the sound they emit. Even if your cat's eyesight is good, these fountains can provide the entertainment that some cats derive from watching a tap drip.
- Add some water or broth to his meals, bearing in mind that if you do this you might have some impact on his dental health, so discuss this with your veterinarian first.
- Make up tuna or meat juice ice cubes by mashing the fish or meat in water and freezing it so you can leave them to melt when needed; this can be a tempting way to encourage your cat to drink more.
- Offer your cat bottled or filtered water to drink.
- If your cat goes out into your garden,

a freshly filled saucer or rain-filled birdbath might attract him.

Adopt whichever strategy appeals most to your cat, but remember that you must keep his preferred source of water constantly available for him and regularly topped up with fresh water.

Left: *Our improved understanding of feline drinking patterns has moved us a long way from the traditional provision of a bowl of water placed by the food dish.*

Below: *Cats often don't enjoy the taste of processed tapwater so will seek out natural water in the outside world.*

Territory

Territory, which was so vital to their ancestors, is in many ways no less important to our cats today. How much they have available, what it contains and what they instinctively feel they need can be crucial to their happiness. Much of your cat's 'daily round' is taken up with activities related to it, and this sometimes puts him at odds with his owner.

Left: Cats devote a significant proportion of their daily 'time budget' to checking up on their territory.

Right: Different vantage points will be used by cats to get a good look at their territory and see that nothing is untoward.

Territoriality

This is the behaviour used by any animal in establishing and defending a territory. You may find it puzzling that your cat is still motivated to display territoriality, even when he is so well provided for, but it proves how instinctive it is for all cats, even though the motivation of different pets varies according to their family history, individual temperament, the space they have, how satisfactory their world is, and their current emotional state. All these factors play a part in determining how much attention each cat devotes to his territory, staking his claim and constantly renewing it.

Even cats that are not overtly aggressive towards intruders may indulge in more territorial behaviour than is obvious at first glance. For instance, much of the head bunting and rubbing you have probably noticed your cat doing on objects that have been recently introduced into your home are part of placing his mark – in effect, he is clearly labelling this change in the physical layout of his territory as his.

Of course, whatever it is that has been introduced to the cat's territory – from a new item of furniture to a briefcase you take to work everyday – will also have its own particular scent. When you remember how important odour is to all cats, it will come as no surprise to learn that the scent profile of the item must also be changed to coincide with that of the feline occupant of your home.

What a territory contains matters

When you look at your cat's environment, bear in mind that the resources it contains are no less significant to him than the equivalent items were to his forebears, although they may not be exactly the same. We may provide food, a comfortable bed, chairs for resting, company and toys, but our cats still need to make their own decisions about how much, or how many, objects they have access to, when and where. Deprived of a sense of control, many pets become severely stressed, particularly when it comes to their territory.

Despite the easier life your cat has compared with his ancestors, it's quite usual to see him regularly patrolling his domain, and, in the light of prevailing circumstances, indulging in some, or all, of the behaviours that firmly stamp this particular patch as his own.

Things change over time, too. Scent marks decay, and other cats pass that way, leaving odour markers that have to be obliterated and visual markers freshened up. And so the cycle of patrolling, inspection, marking, exploring for new opportunities is repeated endlessly, just as it was for your cat's ancestors, who were driven by basic survival imperatives.

In view of this, it also makes sense that providing elevated observation points for your cat is important. We have all seen cats trying out different positions in trees or on fences, shed roofs, pergolas, children's climbing frames or windowsills. What better place could there be to survey and become familiar with what's theirs than a raised area with a good view? In addition, these are often locations that give the occupier an advantage if active rather than passive territorial defence becomes necessary. At the same time, skulking beneath the branches of a nearby shrub or in a nearby tree offers an opportunity to indulge in the preferred feline strategy of hiding, whether for protection or for stalking, if that's what circumstances dictate.

Territorial concerns

Your cat's territory, whether it's large or small, isn't just one space where every aspect of his life may be undertaken anywhere he happens to be at a particular moment. From the feline perspective, certain functions are appropriately carried out in particular places. Understanding what, where and why is crucial if you are going to understand your cat.

Territorial divisions

An individual cat's territory is divided into three main areas, each of which has a particular significance for him. These are:

- The core area which is, to all intents and purposes, where a cat eats, sleeps and plays (ESP).
- The home range, an area outside the core that is important to the individual cat as a sort of buffer zone between him and other cats.
- The hunting range, an area which often overlaps with the home ranges of other cats.

How large each of these areas is, and how hotly contested, depends to a large extent on the local feline population. It is becoming increasingly common in urban locations, where people are densely packed together and cats are popular pets, to find that some cats can only comfortably have access to a very small garden next to their home. A newcomer to the area may even have the misfortune to discover that resident felines have already carved up his owner's patch, making the process of establishing his claim a stressful and intimidating process, which can, unfortunately, lead to a range of problem behaviours.

The territorial behaviour of cats today is clearly underpinned by the patterns that would have been adopted in their ancestors' world. Females, for example, have smaller ranges than males, which roam further looking for opportunities to mate with as many queens as they can. Most owners these days neuter their cats, which affects how large their ranges are. Neutered cats generally lay claim to smaller areas than their entire counterparts because they don't have the urge to breed. Although, any cat's territorial behaviour depends on inherited traits, temperament and even the age at which he was de-sexed. If you have a sibling pair of cats of differing sex and you neutered them both before their hormones really had any significant effect on them, you might still notice that your male cat roams further from base than his sister.

Some of this behaviour is obviously learned early in life. Sometimes, for instance, people adopt uncastrated males and then neuter them. The removal of their sex hormones may quieten them down to some extent, but if they have been used to travelling away from home, the motivation to wander may not be as subdued as it usually is if such procedures are carried out early in life.

When cats live in a home with another cat or even more than one other cat, whether the group has one core and one home range or whether each cat has a diminished individual territory will depend very much on the personality of the cats and their relationship with each other. This whole issue is being hotly examined at present because many welfare concerns have arisen about the territorial needs of individual cats when they live in a multi-cat home and about how those needs can be best understood and satisfied.

Left: *Even when resting or otherwise occupied, most cats are still aware of what's going on around them.*

Right: *Territories can become hotly contested when houses are built close together and gardens are small.*

Territorial labelling

It is, of course, no good for any cat to establish a territory, large or small, unless he has some means of advertising to others that he has staked his claim. Our clever cats have developed a number of ways of doing this that minimize the need to meet the opposition, which might involve face-to-face confrontation or even more physical defence measures.

Territorial marking

Your cat will use four main ways to mark his territory and advertise his claim :

- Stropping
- Bunting and flank rubbing
- Urine marking
- Middening

Of these, bunting is the most attractive from the human perspective, the others far less so, especially when they are brought indoors. Spraying urine and scratching furniture are common problem behaviours, whereas middening, when your cat leaves faeces exposed in unwanted places, is less common, but they always happen for a reason.

Stropping

Most cat owners are familiar with the sight of their cats stretching out as tall as they can against a vertical structure and raking their claws downwards with some considerable force. The marks they leave on trees, fence posts and sheds as well as on chairs, stairs and doorframes serve a purpose: they are visual signals that say 'this area is mine'. The higher the territorial marks are the more effective they will be. This explains why so many of the scratching posts that owners buy are never used: they're simply too short (and often too unstable) to be of any value or they are in locations that have no meaning for the feline owner of the home.

Just as humans post sentries at significant entrances, exits and borders of their territories so cats leave their marks, both visual and scented. For this reason stropping tends to be seen:

- Near doors leading to outside
- Around entrances to rooms
- On fence posts around the home range
- On trees within the home range

Your cat will even strop near open windows where the air inflow changes the area's scent profile, making him feel somewhat threatened and prompting him to lay down his marker.

It is also not unusual to see significant places along 'trails' within our homes and gardens marked in this way, some cats combine it with other behaviour patterns, such as bunting or even sometimes urine spraying.

Other benefits
The scratching behaviour also benefits the muscles, ligaments and tendons of the fore legs, paws and claws by exercising them. It helps to remove the outer sheaths of the claws, which grow continuously and need to be shed from time to time.

You will probably see your cat stropping when he stretches having just woken up – in much the way we do – to get things into working order and avoid the muscular injuries that can accompany the sudden movement of stiff limbs.

Odours plays a part
Because we know that scent is so significant in the feline world, it will come as no surprise to learn that stropping has an important additional role in leaving odorous messages for other cats and for the 'sender'. When your cat indulges in this activity, he is depositing odours from the scent glands in the skin between his footpads. Needless to say, with our poor olfactory powers we can smell nothing, but these odours advertise ownership both to your cat and to other cats in the neighbourhood.

When stropping becomes a problem
Many owners find the habit of stropping less than endearing. It can even seem malicious and spiteful, especially when precious new items are damaged or when a specially bought scratching post is rejected in favour of the new sofa. However, we should try to realize just how pressurized in territorial terms a cat can feel. He may be having to deal with a new cat, puppy or newborn baby intruding into his space; the comings and goings in his home are creating uncertainty

Right: Stropping is one normal feline behaviour that frequently causes owners problems when it moves indoors.

Left: Far less distressing to owners than stropping is bunting – when cats mark their territory by rubbing against objects.

Scent from his flanks will also be mixed with yours when he wraps himself around your legs, just as he does around table legs or on anything else that smells 'foreign' and needs to be labelled to make it smell familiar. Again, your cat is clearly creating a reassuring community scent that tells him that everything in this important area is securely stamped as familiar and that he belongs among these things.

Signs of tension
If you have more than one cat and they are well bonded to each other, you may also observe them approaching each other and sniffing, first noses, then behinds. This is nothing more than an individual and colony recognition procedure. If they get on well, they will often then indulge in quite a lot of allorubbing (see page 31) and entwining of their tails.

In fact, this type of behaviour can help you work out just how harmonious your multi-cat home really is. If you realize that you never see your cats greeting each other in this way but you do notice that one or both spends a lot of time over-marking where their housemate has already been, your pets may not be as happy living together as you thought. Unfortunately, failing to recognize the tensions in a multi-cat household often leads to even more unsavoury territorial marking behaviour (see urine marking and middening pages 54–5), which can understandably stress owners as much as their pets.

and unpredictability in his world and are inadvertently making him feel stressed; or fastidious cleaning regimes constantly obliterate all the marks he's diligently depositing that make him feel safe and secure.

Emotional uncertainty is a common cause of extra marking in all its forms, and stropping is only one of them.

Bunting and flank rubbing
The habit of bunting is one that often seems endearing, especially when our cats do it to us. It is far less distressing for owners than stropping – unless, of course, repeated efforts in one area leave oily stains. However, as with most things they do, rubbing has a serious purpose for our cats.

The message is clear
You may see your pet making his way around the garden sniffing bushes, shrubs, flower tubs or watering cans at cat height, then very intently pushing against them with his face. The peri-oral glands at the side of the mouth are especially used in this type of marking, and the behaviour will be particularly intensely performed when your cat is responding to the scents previously deposited by another cat – or even a dog or fox – that's been around in his absence. He may then turn round and spray urine if he feels especially vulnerable and needs to reinforce his message and enhance his own sense of security.

There are additional scent glands in the areas between your cat's eye and ear, where you see a baldish band running between the two, and also on the body and around the base of the tail. The glands on his head tend to be pressed into action when your cat bunts other individuals, including you, as well as fixtures, fittings and possessions in your home.

PHEROMONOTHERAPY
Pheromones are the naturally occurring scents that animals use to communicate with each other, and pheromonotherapy is a recognized therapeutic tool that is widely used in programmes aimed at resolving stress-related problem behaviours developed by cats.

Two fractions of the facial scents (F3 and F4) that cats deposit when they bunt both objects and individuals have been isolated, and they are now available commercially. It is not, however, entirely clear how they work, but they certainly have a role to play in reducing feline anxiety. The synthetic analogue of F3 can be helpful with indoor marking problems and it is also recommended to help reduce feline tension in stressful circumstances, such as visits to the veterinary clinic, staying in a cattery or when cats and owners move home. The synthetic analogue of F4 is used in the clinic to try and make the veterinary staff less intimidating for fearful patients.

Left: Cats will sniff their way around the garden to try and pick up the scents of other animals. He will push against plants and flowers with his face to leave his own scent markings.

Above: Carefully observing greeting behaviour – or lack of it – can tell us a lot about feline relationships. Nose touching is a recognition procedure which will move to allorubbing if the cats get on.

Urine marking

Both male and female cats use urine both to mark their territory and to advertise their availability and willingness to mate. Neutered cats of both sexes, however, will also label their range and locations within it in the same way, although, of course, their motivation is territorial not sexual. They will even sometimes use faeces for the same purpose.

What we see

Spraying urine is usually associated with a particular stance: a cat will sniff an area or object and will then turn round and, with tail quivering and hind feet paddling back up to it, squirt small volumes of urine against the vertical surface. This creates a recognizable splash pattern at cat height when the urine dries. Interestingly, when the behaviour is transferred indoors into the core area, which happens as a response to feline stress, some cats adopt a squatting position, which can be confused with urination. In general, however, spraying is performed in the characteristic raised-tail position at the periphery of the cat's home range or along walkways within it.

The information that cats convey in this way is related to:

- Their presence: the urine says 'I belong here' or 'I've just been by so please wait a while to avoid us meeting', which is in line with the species' need to maintain distance between individuals
- Their identity: the scent enables other cats to distinguish individuals and members of feline communities
- Health status and age
- Sex

Middening

This type of marking behaviour is less common than stropping, bunting and spraying urine, and it has only recently been recognized for what it is. Unfortunately, it can occasionally be seen in a cat's core area, much to the understandable consternation of owners. This behaviour is very different from feline elimination, which is usually done discreetly. Middening relates to advertising ownership, so the faecal deposits are there to be seen.

It's evident to anyone who is familiar with feline behaviour, that cats that undertake this sort of marking are behaving very differently from the way they do when they are passing urine and faeces as the waste products of digestion. Just how differently they behave will become apparent when we look at normal elimination in some detail (see pages 62–3).

What does middening involve?

When your cat deploys his faeces in this way he is motivated by a need to mark his territory, and for this reason the excreta are usually found in exposed locations where they will be readily seen by other cats. You might, therefore, find

Above: *Most owners have no trouble accepting urine spraying outside but it's a common cause of distress if it moves indoors.*

Right: *Middening can be used by cats to mark territory and they often do this in exposed locations, such as roof tops, where it will be easily seen by other cats.*

such deposits on the roofs of sheds, outhouses and garages, along the tops of garden walls or in the middle of a lawn or path. Unfortunately, the behaviour, which is usually only seen in the home range, can move indoors, where, for obvious reasons, kitchen work surfaces are a favourite location, although other areas and electrical items can sometimes be targeted.

Unpleasant as this is for any owner to have to deal with, the essential thing is to recognize that when a cat soils his core area, particularly in this way, he is suffering from stress and not setting out to cause people distress. Punishment and negative attitudes on the part of the owner are not only likely to be ineffective but will probably compound the difficulties, making the whole situation worse.

Dealing with middening
Few owners experience middening, but if you are unlucky enough to do so try looking at what is going on in your world from your cat's point of view. Try to identify any factors that

are causing your cat to feel under stress and take steps, if you can, to eliminate them. This will help you to begin to deal effectively – and sensitively – with the situation. It is particularly useful to keep a diary of the problem incidents and anything that happens around that time. Also draw a plan of your home and mark the affected areas. Relating this information to what you have learned about feline behaviour may help you to resolve the situation.

Above: With eyes wide and narrowed, bared teeth and whiskers held stiffly to the side, this cat's facial expression is clearly aggressive and threatening.

Right: This cat's erect tail and ears held back shows that he is alert and in control, while trying to avoid confrontation.

Aggression

The behaviours of stropping, bunting, spraying urine and middening are passive methods of defence. They are intended to keep intruders out and to put distance between your cat and his neighbours, and they can be remarkably effective. However, there are times when they simply aren't enough, at which point active defence may become your cat's only option.

Cats prefer to avoid risk

There are times when aggression is your cat's only option. Most cats, however, are no more gung-ho when it comes to risk than their ancestors were, and even when they are pushed to the limit they will usually try to avoid accidental injury. As a result, most of the often quite upsetting aggression we see is designed for display only and to achieve its aim of putting more distance between cats without the need for actual contact, with all the potential dangers that could entail.

Unfortunately, the strategy doesn't always work, and from time to time we do see cats really setting about each other. Some cats even inflict quite considerable injuries on people, generally because the person has misread or ignored the cats' 'back off and keep away' signals.

Understanding aggression

When it comes to feline aggression you must bear in mind that this is normal behaviour, which was developed by nature. No cat, no matter how aggressive, is actually enjoying 'being nasty' in this way. In addition, the readiness with which and the extent to which any particular cat will use aggression will, like everything else our cats do, be dictated by his personal genetic inheritance, temperament and life history. Some cats react quickly and seem ready to explode with aggression at a moment's notice. Other cats, no matter how threatened or fearful they feel, will find it almost impossible to express their feelings outwardly, preferring instead to do their best to pretend they are invisible and no threat to anyone.

You will quickly discover to which of these two groups your own cat belongs if you take the time to look, listen and learn as you see him responding to everything and everyone in the world around him. Study his body language and compare it with the photographs to work out his emotional state in a range of situations. This will not only help you get to know him better, but will also enable you to protect him from stressful circumstances you may not have realized he found hard to cope with.

If you consider his behavioural history after you've read Chapters 3 and 4 of this book, you might be better able to predict how he will feel about certain events, situations or individuals, and then you will be better able to deal effectively with him when he encounters them.

Signs of aggression

As we have seen, your cat can say a lot before he even opens his mouth to growl, hiss or spit, which are all fairly obvious signs of displeasure or fright. Among the signs of aggression that cats use are:

- Body language: your cat's stance may be tall and erect; the head and tail may be down slightly and the body crouched; the back may be arched, with head down, ears flattened against the head, and the tail held high and pointing down.
- Facial expression: the fine-tuning of feline communication lies in the face – the whiskers can be relaxed, or stiff and held downwards, or held stiffly out to the sides to make the cat look bigger and more menacing.
- Eye contact: widening and narrowing the eyes and dilating and contracting his pupils can make a cat's expression attractive and welcoming or threatening and scary; a prolonged, wide-eyed, pupil-dilated stare is really the last word in the feline 'threat lexicon', and it pays owners and other cats to take note and appropriate action. If others don't back off a cat at this stage of arousal has litte choice but to attack.

Stress and fear

When it comes to active aggression and understanding how your cat might feel in a particular situation, it's important to realize the evolutionary significance of the physiological and psychological stress response. It goes hand in hand with fear and the perception of threat, and it is an important part of the feline world.

Right: After a distressing encounter a cat will often groom himself as a way of calming down.

Below: Reacting appropriately to a potential threat is essential for the survival of any species or individual and flight is the preferred feline choice.

The stress response

It's usual to view stress in a totally negative light. Indeed, it can be harmful if it's unremitting and experienced over a long period, with an individual unable to improve his situation or escape from the pressures. However, we need to remember that no individual and no species would have survived without the ability to react appropriately to a perceived danger when the need arose. To do this:

- The brain must register the potential threat, prime the body for action via the nervous system and think more clearly in order to make good decisions.
- The body must respond by increasing the blood flow to muscles, ligaments, joints and the brain.

In times of stress every system of the body is 'on full alert' – it's not a pleasant sensation, but it's one that most of us are familiar with. It's also one that has kept everyone out of trouble at some time or other.

Then, if the situation resolves itself or the danger passes, the 'action stations' call is followed by 'all clear, stand easy' signals, and the mind, body and emotions relax. This normal, healthy response explains why cats and owners belong to species that have survived the course of evolution.

The four Fs

When your cat is alerted to possible danger, he has, like humans, a choice of potential strategies. 'The four Fs' – flight, fight, freeze and fiddle – will reveal a lot about your cat and show how he feels about the different situations he encounters every day, as well as on those special occasions when something out of the ordinary happens.

- Flight is the preferred feline coping strategy, because, as we've seen, whenever they can cats would rather avoid trouble than face it full on.
- Fight is something your cat will do if he feels that he has no choice or if he wants something really badly – food, if he is starving, for example, or a place on your lap or even making another cat disappear from in front of him, and preferably from his life.
- Freeze is an atypical strategy for a carnivore like our cat, and it is still the subject of much research among feline behaviourists and veterinarians.
- Fiddle refers to the type of displacement behaviours that we often see cats indulge in when they are in a bit of emotional turmoil, properly known as 'motivational conflict', and most owners are only too familiar with cats that suddenly start washing their faces or bodies as they try to look unconcerned.

As humans we might find ourselves chewing our nails, tapping our feet or shuffling the papers on our desks when we have to do something about a situation but don't quite know what. Cats, however, usually start grooming themselves. This is often 'out of context' and can be quite amusing until we realize that they are distressed. For example, if your cat has had a narrow escape – has just avoided a large vehicle, for instance – when he reaches safety at the side of the road or in his garden he may well suddenly sit down and start grooming himself. The behaviour looks bizarre but has a serious purpose – he is trying to reassure and calm himself down.

You will only truly get to know your cat when you are able to read the significance behind all his actions, especially his reactions to everyone and everything he encounters. Bearing in mind these strategies for coping with stress should help you to do so. When you can accurately 'read' your cat you will have a better chance of determining how comfortable he is with his world. As a result you will be able to help him cope better with potentially troublesome situations by, for example, improving his available facilities and altering the styles of interaction everyone adopts with him.

Fitness and knowledge

It's obvious that an ability to respond effectively in any given situation depends on physical fitness and knowing how to put survival tactics into practice. Being aware of all the neighbouring cats, every hiding place and the best potential escape routes in his area will help your cat feel comfortably in control.

Keeping in trim

As humans know only too well, keeping fit depends on taking the appropriate physical exercise for all the activities we may be called upon to perform. The body must be kept constantly in good working order and finely tuned, so that sudden bursts of activity don't result in injury.

This is why, just as we see athletes limbering up, your cat will stretch and yawn when he wakes up, will exercise his claws, fore paws and limbs, readying them for action. If the space and facilities are not available for your cat to run, jump, climb, spring, stretch and amble he'll have difficulty keeping himself in trim, and sudden moves, for whatever reason, will cause injuries, and he will certainly be more likely to put on weight, with the associated medical problems that that entails (see pages 124–5).

Provision for play

Like other young creatures – including children – cats play to learn the skills that they will need in later life. If you have a kitten or a couple of young cats you must make sure that they have plenty of facilities for physical and mental exercise. Young cats need to practise their social skills, too, and it can be a mistake to rely on other pet cats to entertain and teach youngsters all they need to know as well as providing them with opportunities to practise their new skills.

It is also unfair if a newly introduced kitten is allowed to pester an older cat because no one else is entertaining him. For this reason, it is often suggested that anyone with an established cat who is thinking of getting a kitten should, in fact, takes two litter-mates, so that they will entertain each other rather than pursuing the often retreating back of the resident cat. This can work well, but you must monitor the situation carefully and make sure that there are plenty of toys and interesting things for the kittens to do, otherwise they might gang up and make the older pet's life a misery, which can be a problem in a multi-cat home.

Exploration

As we have seen (see pages 46–9), territory, and all it provides, is a crucial factor in feline society, and cats constantly patrol their own territory and cautiously explore further afield. A cat's willingness to look for new opportunities, tentatively exploring the world and making sure that every change in his environment, physical and social, has been registered, has probably saved many a pet's life. This type of behaviour is one of the things that makes cats such appealing company. They need to see what we've introduced into their core area when we return from shopping, and it must be a stony-hearted owner who hasn't smiled at some time or other when a box has been carefully sniffed, bunted and sat in – and then possibly adopted as a preferred resting place for some time afterwards. But the serious side to this is that insensitivity on our part can lead to problem behaviour when too many changes happen in a short time.

ADULTS AND PLAY

Adult cats generally grow out of playing, although they will sometimes indulge in a game, even in harsher free-living conditions than our pets enjoy. However, possibly due to our tendency to neuter our cats, play is often a much more important feature of our cats' lives. Play also performs the additional useful function of providing a release from tension and an outlet for mental or physical frustration. Don't discard the toys just because your cat has become an adult, and make sure that you provide plenty of other opportunities for him to exercise his brain.

Above: *Kittens at play are engaged in the serious process of learning – but that doesn't stop their antics being endlessly entertaining for their owners.*

Left: *A cat's natural curiosity is aroused by new objects, and large boxes offer a great opportunity to explore.*

Toileting behaviour

Owners should try to check their cat's toileting to make sure that he is fit and that all is well. However, this is easier said than done if your cat has free access to outdoors and can choose his own latrine sites. Cats tend to be secretive about this aspect of their behaviour, but it's your responsibility to make sure that there are no signs of diarrhoea, constipation or urinary tract infection.

Cats are sensitive

When it comes to relieving themselves domestic cats certainly live up to their reputation for fastidious behaviour. An owner's failure to understand their need for privacy is a common contributing factor in cases of house soiling, the most frequent problem that pet behaviour counsellors are asked to help with. Like us, cats tend to select latrine sites that are secluded and not unpleasant to spend time in. So, if an area is too public, soiled or smelly it will usually be shunned.

If he has a choice, your cat will prefer not to pass urine or faeces in his core area, which, as we've seen (page 48), is generally his home base, where he eats, sleeps and plays (ESP). Your cat will be especially offended if he is forced by prevailing conditions to eliminate near his food. It makes sense in hygiene terms for him not to contaminate this main area of activity, especially the places where he eats. After all, most people would rather not have dinner in the bathroom. So, we create all sorts of problems for our cats if we expect them to behave differently from us in this respect. Instead, cats seek out sites nearer the periphery of their home range, and once they are satisfied with a particular spot they will tend to return to it.

Maintaining standards

Whether your cat goes outside to relieve himself or uses a tray indoors, if you watch him you will notice that he searches for a suitable spot, expends some effort digging a hole – this sometimes needs to be modified several times before use – then squats to pass urine or often adopts a somewhat higher stance to defecate. Then he will reverse the ritual with dedicated attempts to cover all the waste. He may well sniff carefully, continuing his efforts to hide all his deposits and making a determined effort to mask their smell. This process can be particularly protracted after he's passed faeces, and he's likely to seek an especially private location for this.

CONDITIONS MUST BE RIGHT
What constitutes privacy for a cat will depend largely on the lifestyle of each individual cat. If he has access to outdoors, he is likely to choose an area of established garden with shrubs and mature plants to provide a convenient screen for him to hide behind, away from the eyes of other cats, noisy, playing children, passers-by and so on.

Left: Cats prefer to toilet outdoors in areas of the garden that are overgrown or bushy, affording them the privacy they require.

Far left: A cat will spend some time digging a hole that meets his exacting toilet standards.

Cats seem to feel especially vulnerable when they are defecating, and this is probably because the whole activity takes quite a long time. They are likely to become stressed if they are interrupted or overlooked by people or other cats.

Male and female cats behave in the same way, and both sexes can be readily deterred from going outside in bad weather or if pressure from the local feline population makes sorties outside intimidating. It's always advisable to have emergency facilities available indoors (see pages 64–65), which you should put in a suitable location – just in case.

This is an important issue because many house soiling problems are caused because litter trays are placed in convenient areas that are too busy or public to suit the cat's need for privacy.

When it comes to feline elimination it isn't just a case of where, when and how. Cats are as fastidious about what they dig into as they are about all other aspects of their toileting behaviour, and this has led to some fascinating studies, which have been given impetus by the changing lifestyles of our pets and the recognition that a reluctance to relieve themselves causes a variety of medical as well as behavioural difficulties.

Providing the right conditions

OUR RESPONSIBILITIES

Carefully covering what they eliminate in a natural setting makes sense for cats. It minimizes the contamination of their environment, reduces the likelihood of the transmission of internal parasites and avoids advertising their presence to other animals. That cats remain so fastidious today is part of their attraction for many people.

Our important role, therefore, is to make sure that we provide the right conditions for them to carry out their normal toileting patterns, and we must be aware that our failure in this respect can lead to:

• Faulty learning in kittens.
• House soiling, with elimination in inappropriate places by youngsters and older cats alike.
• An abnormal desire in some cats to relieve themselves on surfaces that cause owners problems, including carpets, human bedding or newspapers and magazines.
• Unnecessary stress for the cats, which may, in turn, result in other medical or emotional problems.

LEARNING FROM THE PAST

Fortunately, we can look at 'natural' feline behaviour to help us provide the right conditions for our cats today,

because we know that cats are fastidious about the substrate – which is what the soil, sand, peat or cat litter, in fact whatever they use to cover their excreta, is called.

Their distant desert-dwelling ancestors obviously used the sand around them as substrate, so it should come

AVOIDING PROBLEM SUBSTRATES

Problems can arise if the litter that you are providing for your cat:

• Produces an unpleasant odour from the feline not the human point of view.

• Is highly perfumed, which may be pleasant for you and your family but is a real deterrent for most cats.

• Is heavy or uncomfortable for cats to rake, dig in or stand on – for example, some of the litters that are based on wood shavings are quite sharp or produce resins when wet that will sting your cat's feet.

as no surprise to find that research confirms that our cats prefer light, dry, granular substrates that are pleasant for them to rake up with their paws. These are the same paws that cats sometimes use to investigate their food, whether it is alive or not, which is another reason they are unlikely to be attracted to substrates that are unpleasant to touch, because they are, for example, cold and wet or already heavily contaminated, especially with faeces. Cats find it particularly offensive if they are forced to share latrine facilities so that the contamination is communal rather than individual.

CHOOSING A SUBSTRATE
Although every cat is an individual – in this as in every other respect – it

seems certain that the type of litter they generally prefer is light, granular, clumping and clay like.

Your cat is less likely to develop inappropriate eliminatory habits if he is provided with a substrate that he finds personally acceptable. This has become more of an issue as the range of cat litters that are available commercially has increased. Some, although highly artificial in nature, are light and granular, with a tendency for the soiled patches to clump together, and they absorb odours well – the characteristics of the original sandy soil your cat's forebears were used to. These types of substrates, while being significantly different from the sand or light clay that most cats prefer, are still within the range of acceptability.

Above: Unsurprisingly pet cats' litter preferences reflect the sandy terrain in which their ancestors behaviour first developed.

Left: Kittens quickly learn to use a litter tray, fulfilling their natural instinct to cover their excreta.

Instilling good habits

Even though you do your best to choose the most appropriate substrate for your cat, he might still prefer what was available in the earliest weeks of his life. This is when kittens learn appropriate behaviour, as long as they have the facilities available for them to do so, and it's always worth asking the breeder or previous owner what your kitten or cat has become used to, so you can make sure you continue with the same substrate.

Introduce change gradually

Because cats will use a particular substrate if it's all they have available to maintain their typical fastidious habits, providing a choice of litters that seem more suitable to the species' natural preferences may be a good idea if you think that the original substrate may be unsuitable. Changing the substrate to which your cat is accustomed can be difficult, however.

Never make an abrupt change from one type of litter to another: that is, frankly, a recipe for disaster and could lead to some of the problems outlined on page 64. It's much better to offer a choice, so that you can see which is most acceptable to your cat, then gradually switch over.

Litter depth matters

The nature of the substrate and making sure that the tray is regularly cleaned and supplied with fresh litter are not the only factors that have been studied. Your cat is also going to be affected by the quantity of litter in his tray.

Trials in which cats were offered a choice of identical trays with the same litter but in differing amounts – so that it was either shallow or deep – confirm what we might expect: cats like to be able to cover up their excreta really well. Anyone who has watched a cat trying, often with some apparent desperation, to bury deposits when there is insufficient material available will be able to confirm the findings of the trials. You might feel that your cat actually suffers some distress when conditions are not to his liking. Interestingly, however, it seems that the same cats were not so fussy when it came to hiding their urine, but this again makes sense if we think about the accepted purpose in feline terms of the whole process: faeces are a much more significant contaminant than urine.

Going outside isn't enough

It might seem as if owners of cats that have free access to outdoors really don't need to bother with such issues as preferences and amounts of cat litter, but this assumption would be wrong. Providing the right conditions and materials can be just as much an issue for cats with outside latrine areas as it is for those cats that remain indoors. In fact, a particular problem, especially in built-up urban areas, is the current minimalist design trend, where gardens have become little more than 'made-over' outdoor living areas for people. The modern passion for decking, patios, water features and containers has robbed cats of the suitable latrine areas that were once ubiquitous.

So, whether your cat has an indoor life or free access to outdoors, do look at what he has at his disposal and try to work out how satisfactory and appealing his options are in this respect. Improve them if you need to, and if you're not

sure, offer him an educated choice and see what he prefers – he'll soon let you know what he likes best. If on the other hand, you don't give him the right latrine facilities for his personal preferences, you could be inadvertently storing up problems for your cat – and possibly therefore for yourself – later on.

OUTDOOR SOLUTIONS

Increasing numbers of owners are building dedicated outdoor latrines for their cats, and this isn't difficult to do. At the very least, you should consider regularly digging over a couple of areas in your flower beds to make them pleasant for your cat to use. Don't forget to remove any faecal contamination, and perhaps adding some good-quality sand to improve the soil's composition and drainage could make all the difference to his life.

Above: Owners who fail to provide suitable latrine facilities for their cats, whether outside or indoors, often pay the price when house soiling problems develop.

Left: A dedicated cat latrine in the garden could be the solution if patios, decking or other features have reduced your cat's choices.

Cats at rest

After all the strenuous activity of the daily feline round, it's no wonder that our cats have to allow themselves a moment or two for rest. Or, as most owners would testify with a certain degree of envy, cats spend many hours doing nothing interspersed with short bursts of action, after which they rest again.

Left: *With paws tucked in, this cat is enjoying a light sleep but will still be alert to any noises that may indicate a threat or potential prey.*

Right: *Contentedly curled up in the sunshine, keeping warm and conserving energy, this cat is enjoying paradoxical, or deep, sleep.*

Resting and sleeping

A high-protein diet, rich in calories, allows your cat the luxury of doing very little for much of his day – most cats spend about 16 hours doing not very much, as it happens. It would be a mistake to regard resting and sleeping as times when absolutely nothing happens, however. The purpose of this down-time is to allow your cat to conserve his energy, so that if he were dependent on his own efforts to find and catch food he would be better prepared for the short bursts of energy that hunting requires. Finding sheltered, cosy spots also means that less energy is expended during resting and sleeping in keeping warm. Every cat owner will be familiar with their cat's predilection for the airing cupboard or

wardrobe, the fireside or even under the duvet. Owners whose cats have access to the garden will have seen them sleeping in a sunny corner, dozing on a warm shed roof or curled up in a shady nook on a hot, sunny afternoon.

It also makes sense that our cats are more active at night when their prey species are on the move under cover of darkness, although this pattern does vary with geography. Many of today's cats sleep more during the night than their free-living cousins, but even so their preference for activity at dusk and dawn frequently puts them on a collision course with owners, who would really prefer to recharge their batteries for the next working day than play. As a result,

some authorities are adamant that cats should not be allowed into bedrooms. However, it's really a matter of choice, and many cat lovers regard the odd enforced early waking as a small price to pay for the comfort of a warm cat at the bottom of the bed.

Getting comfortable

After finding the right place – something that cats are good at – they usually rest in one of two postures. The position known as sternal recumbency involves them crouching or half-sitting on their chests with their paws tucked in. Otherwise, they lie on their sides, their bodies either curled tightly or, if the weather is warm, in a more relaxed fashion, with their tails wrapped around and under the chin.

Phases of feline sleep

As with humans, a cat's sleep is a more active process than it might at first appear, and it consists of two phases: light or slow-wave sleep, which is interspersed with bouts of deeper REM or paradoxical sleep (see page 70).

Light or slow-wave sleep

Between 9 and 12 hours or more of your cat's daily sleep is the slow-wave kind. During it, your cat is still alert to danger, because hearing continues to be as acute as ever. The main characteristics of this type of sleep are:

- Breathing and heart rates decrease
- Blood pressure is lowered
- Pupils of the eye contract
- Skeletal muscles are still

In addition, the third eyelid (nictitating membrane) protrudes from the inner corner of the eye to slide across the eyeball, and this is why, if your cat is suddenly woken, he might at first almost appear blinded by a white skin across his eyes, which can be a source of consternation to some new owners, although it soon retracts to normal once the cat is awake.

REM sleep

Rapid eye movement (REM) or paradoxical sleep is the sleeping phase in which humans are known to dream. It is called paradoxical sleep because although it appears to be deep, it is characterized by brain wave patterns that are similar to those experienced during wakefulness, by heavier breathing and by the rapid eye movements that give it its alternative name.

Obviously, it is impossible to be certain if cats do dream during this type of sleep, even from brain wave recordings, because they can't tell us. However, they do exhibit some behaviour during this phase that suggests that they process information and may relive experiences at such times.

Characteristics of REM sleep

REM sleep alternates with longer bouts of slow-wave sleep (see page 69), and about 30 per cent of your cat's total sleep is the REM type. It has the following characteristics:

- It occurs within 10–30 minutes after your cat falls asleep
- The eyes flick in rapid movements of 8–30 at a time
- The ears twitch
- Paws and claws move rhythmically
- Whiskers move irregularly
- Breathing is irregular
- The tail may twitch
- The tongue may flicker
- The pupils dilate

If your cat is woken from this type of sleep when he is nicely settled on your lap he may seem disorientated and cling to you with his claws before jumping down to gather himself – this is normal, although you may bear the scars to prove it happened.

Lack of sleep

Like their owners, cats will become irritable if they are deprived of sleep for any length of time, which is worth bearing in mind if you have lots of visitors who insist on fussing over, playing with and generally keeping your cat busy when he would normally be resting. The amount of sleep an individual needs tends to decrease throughout life, so older cats generally show fragmented sleep patterns with significantly less deep sleep.

Waking up ritual

When your cat wakes up, he is likely to do so from slow-wave sleep. He will stretch and possibly do a bit of stropping on nearby objects such as chairs, or carpeted steps in preparation for his next bout of activity.

Grooming and personal hygiene

You have probably noticed that when your cat is awake he spends a lot of his time attending to his appearance. Their suppleness allows cats to reach most of their bodies with their tongue, which has backward-pointing spines (papillae) that make it an effective comb for removing dead hair, shed skin debris and parasites.

In hot weather grooming can also help to cool a heated cat by spreading saliva on to his coat to dry by evaporation. This is an especially useful adaptation, because cats have sweat glands only on the soles of their feet, which means that the only evidence that your cat sweats that you are likely to see is damp paw prints on the veterinary consultation table.

Left: After a good snooze a cat's long slow stretch readies him for action and helps avoid injury if sudden rapid movement is required.

Right: Once awake, your cat will spend some time grooming, an activity that is both practical and calming.

Reading your cat

Cats are subtle 'signallers' but do use body language and facial expression to convey how they're feeling. Their expressive mobile ears, whiskers and tails enhance their visual repertoire, which can help us understand our pets' emotional state. But remember the whole picture counts and one particular aspect taken in isolation can be misleading.

BODY POSTURE
- Loose limbed, causal gait indicates a relaxed confident pet
- Slow, cautious movements with taut muscles suggest an alert cat, perhaps hunting (prey, toys or other cats) or having spotted a potential threat
- Low crouched position or tense straight back leading down to a tail tucked under his body demonstrates a pet is anxious
- Raised hair (piloerection) along an arched back, 'bottle brush' tail, ears turned slightly back and flat indicates the 'Halloween or witch's' cat is fearful
- If retreat is impossible he'll lower his body ready to roll over and defend himself with teeth and claws
- Tensely tall, raised rump stance with tail extended backwards, ears held forwards or slightly twisted behind, suggests a confident cat using intimidation. Prior to attack he'll block the way, stare through constricted pupils and his whiskers will be stiffly extended forward
- Rolling sideways or on his back with floppy limbs and tail, or stretched out with his 'toes tucked under' indicates a relaxed and happy pet

EAR POSITION
- Pricked up and forward suggests an alert but untroubled pet
- Stiffened and lowered indicates anxiety or fear
- Threatened felines protect their ears, so flat against the head is an entirely defensive position
- Rotated slightly around to the back and somewhat flat together with other aggressive indicators, signals an assertive individual who may attack

CATS' EYES
Emotions and light affect feline eyes.

- Narrowed eyes, constricted pupils suggests bright light or assertive/aggressive intent
- Relaxed face, moderately wide eyes, constricted pupils indicates an interested confident cat
- Fairly narrow eyes, dilated pupils signals apprehension
- Wide open eyes with dilated pupils indicates low intensity light/interested observation/high arousal as in play or fear
- Drooping eyelids show a relaxed, sleepy cat

WHISKERS
Cats' whiskers are very mobile, moving quickly as their activities and emotions change. So they are:

- Extended out to the side and downwards by a confident, alert cat

- Thrust forward and stiffened during play, hunting or intimidation
- Gently droopy when a pet relaxes
- Pulled backwards to protect them by a fearful, threatened cat

TAIL SIGNALS

The feline tail tip moves independently but beware unlike canine tail wagging this sign in cats is generally distance increasing not reducing!

- Horizontal or half lowered is the normal tail position, a cat in 'neutral'
- Straight up, often kinked at the tip is a greeting to other cats and people, frequently accompanied by bunting and rubbing on familiar individuals
- Arched back over his body a cat's tail indicates a desire to reduce distance between himself and others, for example when familiar cats and kittens play
- Rhythmically twitching, particularly the tip, from side to side indicates arousal and agitation. It may be positive when a pet is excited or negative when he's lashing his tail in response to threat
- The tail will be fluffed right up (bottle brush) into a downward U or curled out of danger around his tense lowered back end when a cat is presented with danger
- Held straight out behind a tense cat who's staring at an adversary generally means this is a confident individual who may soon attack
- Drooping or curled comfortably round a relaxed body means 'all's well and I'm resting'

Right: Their cat's friendly tail up greeting often bonds owners even more firmly to a treasured pet.

Left: Putting the whole picture together – flattened body posture, lowered ears, whiskers thrust forward – it is easy to read that this cat is feeling threatened and may attack.

GENETICS AND PERSONALITY

As we have seen, the behaviour patterns that helped your cat's ancestors to thrive underlie everything he does today. During the course of domestication some traits have been modified by close proximity to people, other cats and easier living. So you may wonder why, if the behaviour of all cats is basically the same, they differ from each other in lots of ways. The reason is that numerous forces work together to affect the way our individual pets look as well as how they relate to their surroundings and to everyone around them. Your cat's appearance, attitudes and behavioural traits are the product of interaction between his genetic inheritance, his individuality or 'personality' and his experiences, and these are the subjects we look at next.

Inheritance is the key

All of us, our cats included, inherit a range of traits that affect everything from our outward appearance to the way we view the world and how we react to new, exciting or frightening things. Genes dictate our basic behaviour, whatever our species, but this influence isn't entirely straightforward.

Genetics are not the whole story

The individual character of any pet is shaped by a number of influences, the contribution from any one being modified, or accentuated, by the effects of the others.

The often-debated 'nature versus nurture' argument applies just as much to our cats as to any of their owners. Some of your cat's behaviour has come to him from his forebears, in addition to which he has inherited characteristics from each of his parents, although some traits will be more dominant than others and some more subdued or even completely hidden. Indeed, if you know his mother and observe your pet interacting with his siblings, you may be able to pick out any family traits he exhibits. Similarly, if you've had a litter with your queen and kept a kitten, the offspring may be uncannily like their parent when they achieve adulthood – or may be not.

Left: *As kittens grow it's always fascinating to see the effects of inheritance and experience as their behaviour matures and their personalities develop.*

Right: *A timid kitten may have inherited his cautious characteristics from his parents.*

On the other hand, even two siblings, despite sometimes being as physically indistinguishable as human identical twins raised together, when adopted into the same home will not necessarily behave in exactly the same way as each other. In fact, predicting how cats will turn out is often as troublesome as forecasting the weather.

You may observe this yourself if you've acquired two sibling kittens – double the trouble but double the fun – and often it takes a while for their individual temperaments to emerge. When they do, however, they may be completely alike, but it's not unusual to find litter-mates with distinctly differing personalities.

Like father, like son

Research has looked in detail at paternal characteristics that later emerge in the tomcat's offspring, and the studies have been conducted so that they exclude the possible effects of the queen's nurturing style and focus instead on the father's temperamental traits. As the tomcat has no part in raising the kittens, his influence can only be inherited genetically, not learned by observation after birth. Boldness has been a particularly targeted 'genetic expression', because it is distinct and more easily quantifiable than other, more subtle traits that are harder to observe. The results have shown that the male's character does indeed affect his offspring, something that was previously debated.

Not all inheritance is helpful

The tomcat can bequeath a bold, outgoing character to his offspring, but equally easily he could pass on to them a tendency to display timidity and fearfulness. This matters because the lives of fearful animals are often undermined by chronic stress, which upsets their emotional equilibrium and can adversely affect their overall wellbeing. Such cats are also often disappointing and unsuitable pets, because aggression is commonly motivated by fear, making handling them risky. This is why breeders carefully choose both parents when they are planning to mate cats.

As owners, we need to be very careful about where we get our cats from, or our expectations of what they can cope with may be unfair and lead to difficulties for us and the cats. Many problem behaviours develop as a result of people acquiring pets from backgrounds that don't properly prepare the cats for their destined lives as pets. Often the intentions are good – as when people re-home feral cats when they are more than a few weeks old.

If you're still wondering where to get your cat don't decide until you've read the next chapter. It pays to take time deciding upon the best source of pet for you. The happiest relationships are generally based upon finding the pet whose genetic inheritance, early upbringing and temperament best fit him for your circumstances.

Each cat is unique

In addition to his genetic inheritance from both his ancestors and his parents, each cat develops an individuality that makes him 'himself'. This is impossible to define but explains why even two identical siblings raised in exactly the same way in the same environment cannot be guaranteed to think, feel and act as if they were one.

Left: Persians have a tolerant personality that makes them suitable as pets for young children.

Far left: Even with pedigree cats it can be difficult to predict exactly 'who' will emerge when a pet is fully grown as so many factors are at play.

Recognizing personalities

Some scientists feel uncomfortable with the idea that animals have 'person-ality'. Pointing to our suspect tendency of anthropomorphism (attributing human characteristics to animals), they insist on referring to feline individuality instead. However, opinions are changing, with more people now believing that it's legitimate to talk of cats having 'personalities'.

Why personality matters

Whichever expression we choose – personality or feline individuality – cat lovers see characteristics and foibles associated with particular pets that certainly seem to deserve the label 'personality trait'. In fact, it's accepted practice these days to assign temperamental traits to certain pedigree breeds. Because these cats are deliberately selected from a relatively small gene pool, they're more inclined to uniformity than non-pedigree cats, whose genetic inheritance is so much broader. Particular behavioural aspects become concentrated in pedigree breeds, and failing to recognize specific breed personality traits can lead to problems.

Owners sometimes choose a breed on grounds of fashion or appearance, for example, and they may be unaware that their lifestyle is not really suitable for a recognized behavioural trait that is associated with that type of cat. Unrealistic expectations about how their pet will cope with the way they live can impose unfair pressures, with consequences for their

cat's emotional wellbeing. Some of the Oriental breeds – Burmese and Siamese, for instance – are bright, extrovert, outgoing, inquisitive and often rather 'needy' of attention. It's part of their charm, but for owners with busy lives these are not a particularly suitable choice. Such cats can be lonely when they are left alone, and frustration and boredom can lead them into trouble, such as electric cable chewing and wool eating.

Other cats, like the Russian Blue, are generally somewhat shy and retiring. Although this is part of their attraction for many owners, such a behavioural trait makes them a less than ideal choice for children, whose joy in having a cat comes from being able to cuddle and hug it, whether the cat is keen or not. Indolent, more tolerant Persians may be a better choice in these circumstances, as long as parents are prepared for the coat maintenance they require. Despite their usually equable temperaments though, like any pet cat they do need to have been properly introduced to children in their early weeks when they were most receptive to learning to 'love' them in return.

Personality counts

If your cat is a pedigree you'll no doubt enjoy seeing how like his breed standard personality he turns out to be. However, the expectations that some people have that the temperament of their pedigree cat will be exactly like the description in a book they've read can certainly be misplaced. Other factors are always at work in shaping an individual cat's behaviour. However, yours may well be a non-pedigree cat, so you will know what a mistake it is to assume that less blue-blooded felines are lacking in personality.

Like us, some cats have strong personalities, whereas others are more restrained. Bold, outgoing, sociable felines live alongside those less inclined to stray far from home and those that are generally more self-contained and independent. Undoubtedly, one of the most pleasurable aspects of cat owning is watching as your particular feline companion's individual qualities emerge and as he develops the funny little habits that make him unique.

Nature or nurture

Genetics and individuality are not the only determining forces at work in shaping your cat's behaviour. The circumstances each cat finds himself in will determine a lot of what he does from day to day, and they will also have an influence on his character, and his temperament.

Early days count

What happens early on in any cat's life has a really significant effect on his ability to form relationships with humans and other pets, including cats. During his first few weeks your cat's brain will have developed quickly. Initially immature, it was very receptive to the effects of all the new experiences he had. The people, other animals and general environmental conditions he encountered would have helped to shape his responses to anyone or anything he meets throughout the rest of his life, including you and your home.

As long as he was not frightened, the more a kitten learned about a person, pet, object or even a noise, such as a crackling fire or washing machine, during his early weeks, the more he will be able to take these sights and sounds in his stride. As he grows, if something is entirely novel to him and he can't relate it to anything he is already familiar with, your cat may well perceive it as being a threat. It won't matter that it's a harmless, inanimate domestic item or a cat-friendly person of a different sex, age group or ethnic background from the people he grew up with. When their friendly overtures seem to cause panic in a cat they're trying to win over, it can be really hard for any cat lover not to feel hurt and rejected.

At times like this it's important to remember that his inclination to flee may have little to do with us but it does say an awful lot about what did, or did not happen, to the cat early on in his life.

Left: Sensitive and appropriate handling in his first few weeks is essential to produce a happy, well balanced and satisfying pet cat.

Right: Playing with your cat from an early age will accustom him to a range of toys and create a strong bond with you.

Really knowing your cat

It should be obvious that the more you know about your cat's beginnings the better you will be able to understand what he does now. This should help you anticipate his likely reactions to new, exciting or potentially frightening, people or things. Such information will help you to help your cat cope with all sorts of possible stressors, the term for anything animate or inanimate that arouses and distresses our feline companions.

Don't worry, however, if you have rescued a cat and know little about what happened to him as a kitten or later in his life if he came to you as an adult. Once you start to live together, careful observation of what he does and how he reacts to things will probably help you piece together his behavioural history and deal with him as sensitively as you can both now and in the future.

Sadly, of course, any cat can have the best possible start only to find that his life later takes a negative turn that undermines how he views and reacts to people and their world. This is why we all – breeders, owners and professionals alike – bear such a heavy responsibility with regard to our cats' welfare.

We will all have a better chance of knowing the cat, or cats, that share our homes and bring us such joy in our everyday activities if we make an effort to find out all we can about them and:

- Understand their basic species behaviour
- Know about particular breed or family traits that each cat is likely to inherit
- Respect the individuality of each cat
- Take account of what happened to each cat both in the early weeks and subsequently

YOUR CAT'S DEVELOPMENT

Your cat's behaviour is the result of all his systems working together. The major sense organs and nerve endings all over his body – in his skin, ligaments, joints and muscles, for instance – send information to his brain. This important organizational centre makes the 'executive decisions' that determine how your cat will behave in any situation in which he finds himself. The brain influences his behaviour by sending out messages via the nerves and hormones. It controls everything he does, and it develops its ability to function well as a result of everything your cat encounters. The early months are particularly important, and looking at your cat's developmental stages will help explain why.

Mammalian development

The offspring of many prey animals need to take evasive action if they are faced with predators soon after they're born. If they don't, they won't survive long. Unlike your cat, these young animals are fairly mature when they arrive in the world. This is known as precocial development, and it contrasts with the altricial pattern, which means that much more development occurs after the animal's birth.

Instinctive and learned behaviour

A lot of your cat's behaviour will be instinctive, but he will also learn a lot by observing what his mother and siblings do, as well as experimenting and exploring himself when the time is right. It's important, therefore, that people who look after a pregnant queen should provide the appropriate conditions for her to demonstrate efficiently to her offspring how they should act, or they will be at a disadvantage. Nevertheless, no matter how attentive a mother she is, her kittens may never learn to behave in a way that makes them satisfying pets when they grow up. In addition, if she is fearful of people or stressed by her environment, she may not be a good role model for her young.

Clearly, therefore, breeders and owners play an important part in the way that cats develop, and we let them down if we don't get things right. This is just as true for a family pet's once-in-a-lifetime litter as it is for those kittens that are raised commercially for showing and for sale. If we play our part well, breeding only from well-adjusted parents and making sure that the kittens' environment and early experiences are as ideal as possible, they will grow up to become healthy, behaviourally balanced and rewarding pets. If we get things wrong, the kittens may find life in close proximity to people and all the paraphernalia with which we fill our homes stressful.

Sadly, many of the problem behaviours that later emerge in our feline companions can be traced back to inadequate environments or poor handling in the crucial early stages, and if we look at the phases our cats go through as they grow and develop behaviourally it's not hard to see why.

Pregnancy and birth

If you have a litter with your pet or adopt a pregnant queen, consult your veterinarian about the health and management issues involved in her care. She will need a specially formulated diet to keep her well and to enable her kittens to develop safely. The overall aim is to provide a balanced diet, feeding extra calories when they are needed but making sure that the pregnant queen keeps fit and avoids putting on excess weight.

Your cat's girth will, of course, increase, especially towards the latter half of the gestation period (pregnancy) of around 65 days. She will become less agile and energetic as her abdomen expands, and her behaviour will also change. Some cats become more affectionate, but others prefer independence. If yours is a multi-cat home, you may well find that your queen reacts less equably than normally when she is with the other cats, preferring solitude in preparation for her kittens' arrival.

As the time of their birth approaches she will probably be restless, warning you that the birth is imminent. She may adopt the nesting box you've carefully prepared and placed in a quiet location, but she's just as likely to seek out somewhere for herself – which may not be nearly as convenient for you.

For most cats, labour generally proceeds smoothly, with the kittens arriving at fairly regular intervals and the mother taking care of them without assistance. She usually indicates that all her kittens have arrived by settling down, having a drink and perhaps something to eat. However, if you feel concerned at any stage during pregnancy or birth you should immediately contact your veterinarian for advice.

Right: The birth of kittens is an exciting event in any household, and it's a time when a fine balance needs to be struck between solicitous care of the queen and obtrusive observation that will stress her.

Left: Towards the end of her pregnancy, a queen will be less agile and may prefer to spend more time alone before the birth of her kittens.

Developmental stages

The main stages of a kitten's early life take only a few weeks, but they have a lasting and indelible effect on the adult cat. It's possible to see in a cat's adult behaviour the influences that shaped the kitten's upbringing.

Above: Newborn kittens may be relatively helpless but they are still learning all the time.

Right: Exploring new environments and meeting new people all help to socialize a young kitten to life in the home.

The pre-natal or gestation period

It might seem unlikely that your cat was learning while he was snug in his mother's womb, but although there is still much to discover, it's clear that this isn't simply wasted time. What the mother cat eats now has some influence on the future taste preferences of her offspring, and unborn kittens are aware of sound and may also respond to touch.

Neo-natal period

The neo-natal period lasts from the kitten's birth to ten days of age. Like all kittens, your cat was born with closed eyes, and his ears were folded over, preventing him from hearing. During this period he will have done little except feed and sleep. He will have used their smell to locate his mother and litter-mates and the essential warmth they provided. During this phase, too, it's the queen who initiates suckling, and she will stimulate her kittens to eliminate by licking around their rear ends.

Transitional period

This period lasts from ten days old to three weeks. The physical changes your cat underwent now will have been accompanied by developments in his nervous system, so during this time your cat would have begun to regulate his own body temperature, start to balance and coordinate better and orientate towards the sounds he had previously only just been aware of.

The importance of socialization

Your cat will have experienced a period of rapid physiological and behavioural development between the ages of two and seven weeks. What he experienced then is likely to influence the way he behaves now, no matter what age he is. This stage is called the socialization and habituation period, and it's a time when things really begin to change. The people your cat will have encountered during this important phase of his life and the experiences he had will have provided him with a template, as it were, against which he can measure anyone or anything he comes across now and in the future. If the comparisons are favourable, because he had pleasant and non-threatening early encounters, he will be able to take them in his stride.

If, on the other hand, something or someone frightened him during the socialization period, anything that resembles the object of fear may well be stressful for him in later life. Equally, if he met only a narrow range of people and had little exposure to a normal home – if, for example, he was raised in a cage in an outdoor cattery – he might find lots of people and things really threatening. Imagine that your cat was exclusively reared by a single, middle-aged woman or by a couple of young women, so he didn't have any opportunities to meet men or children until he was older. Now, when he comes across adult men or noisy children they might seem like alien monsters to him, even though they're kind and want to be friends. No one has to do anything nasty. Just wanting to stroke or pick up a cat that didn't meet anyone from a particular sex, age or ethnic group during the socialization phase can be enough to distress him. This is why, when meeting an unfamiliar cat, being aware of who and what he is used to helps us to adopt a sensitive approach.

SOCIALIZATION AND HABITUATION
Socialization is the process by which your cat learns about his own identity, people and other pets – if he was brought up with dogs, for instance. Habituation is the process by which he becomes accustomed to all the potentially scary things he will find in his environment, such as noisy electrical appliances.

Producing a socialized cat

Perhaps surprisingly, it really doesn't take a lot to produce a thoroughly socialized – 'bomb-proof' – kitten that has had all the necessary preparation to grow up into a well-adjusted pet that is at ease with his world and everything it contains. A little knowledge and sensitive, diligent handling is all that's required. Care is needed though because over-enthusiasm has the potential for undermining our efforts.

Good socialization

To make sure that her kittens grow into well-adjusted cats, a mature, single woman could easily ask her friends and neighbours to visit. If these people gently handle the kittens they shouldn't be frightened later in kittenhood or as grown-up cats when they meet men and children of various ages and different appearances – men with beards, for instance, or youngsters with spectacles.

There are three main areas that need to be included in any socialization programme to get the most out of this important life stage so that kittens are prepared to cope with anyone and anything they come across in their adult lives.

First, from the age of just two weeks, kittens should get used to being gently handled (touched, lifted, restrained) by:

• People of both sexes and a wide range of ages; this should begin with the people the queen is happiest with, such as, say, adult females, if she has been handled mostly by women, leaving little children until last

• People of a range of appearances, such as men with beards or someone in uniform
• People from different ethnic groups
• A minimum of four people handling the kittens for 15–40 minutes every day (this small amount of contact can make a really significant difference)

People should handle the kittens in the queen's presence if she is a bold and sociable cat, and she will be a good role model for her offspring. It's also helpful to handle each kitten in the presence of his siblings, which will boost his confidence as long as the other kittens are not overly timid or fearful.

Then kittens need:

• Appropriate exposure to other pets
• A complex but not stressful environment
• A range of appropriate toys
• Good exercise facilities
• Suitable scratching facilities

KITTEN KINDERGARTEN

Originally developed in Australia by a veterinary behaviourist, the concept of 'kitten kindergartens' is spreading. Their aim is to reduce the number of cats relinquished because of behaviour problems by familiarizing young kittens in a positive way with the:

- Veterinary clinic, where they're held

- The procedures they're likely to encounter at the clinic

- Healthy kittens of a similar age

In addition, owners have the opportunity to discuss health care and behavioural issues at an early stage when any difficulties can be most easily resolved.

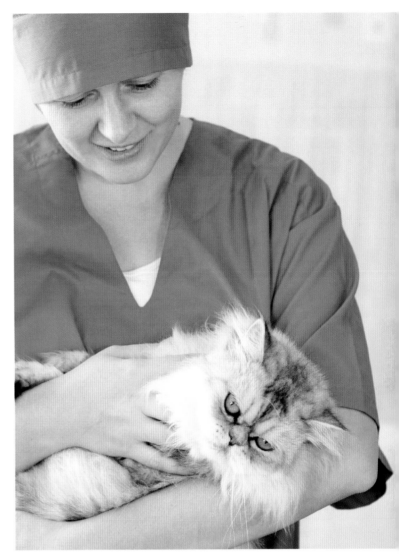

Right: *Familiarizing kittens with the people and procedures at the vets helps them to be relaxed on future visits.*

Left: *A mother's care and attention benefit a young kitten's early experiences in different environments, helping them cope with similar situations in adulthood.*

- Adequate and appropriate toileting facilities
- Non-frightening exposure to the domestic environment, or, if that's not possible, good-quality sound recordings of, for example, electrical equipment, children playing, babies crying and dogs barking

Finally, your kitten needs to be gently and carefully introduced to:

- The range of procedures that veterinary inspections include, such as checking ears, looking under tails and pretending to clip claws
- The catflap, if there is one

Changing views

The socialization and habituation periods used to be called 'critical' periods. The word 'sensitive' is now preferred, because these aren't exactly once-and-for-all opportunities, although we can rarely be so effective later on in a young cat's life. They are the best 'windows of opportunity' we have in which to influence the way our cats will see the world and everything in it. Therefore, this is definitely the best chance we get to do the right things, because our cat's ability to learn is never likely to be quite so sensitive again.

Exceptions prove the rule

There is an interesting exception to this rule. It's not quite clear how, but later in life a previously not very well-socialized cat that experiences a period of acute stress or a serious illness that requires a lot of nursing, can sometimes go through another socialization experience, as it were. This can change his formerly negative attitudes towards being near people if the cat missed out on socialization the first time round. However, as any experienced owner who's had to administer a lot of treatment to their cat will know, under such circumstances cats more commonly come to view people with deep suspicion. It's also unethical, as well as foolish, to deliberately stress any 'antisocial' cat just in the hope of reversing his emotional response to handling and this option should not be artificially reproduced.

Mobility and learning

Of course, none of these important behavioural developments could possibly happen unless a kitten's physical development was also moving on smoothly. Your kitten will have been growing rapidly, and by the age of four weeks he will have learned about himself and been introduced to his new world and all it contains, including the other two- and four-legged individuals he is being brought up with.

Temperature regulation
– a small milestone

By the time he is about four weeks old your kitten will be able to hear and see to some degree. He will also be better at regulating his own temperature, an important advance because it reduces the risk of an exploring kitten getting chilled, which can be life threatening in the early weeks. It's amazing to think that your kitten's independence and ability to discover all sorts of new and exciting things could be enhanced by such a seemingly inconsequential development.

When he is about three weeks old your kitten will still be suckling his mother's milk and will stay close to the nest, but the onset of temperature regulation will allow him to move safely away, and he will start to eat tiny amounts of solid food as well as continuing to suckle. He will then really start to explore his surroundings, and in natural circumstances, it's at this point that the queen will begin to teach her kittens about the important business of food procurement. A free-living cat will bring prey back to the nest, and, because she will not want to risk a potential meal hurting her little ones or this novel, unpredictable object frightening her kittens, their first encounters will be with dead animals.

Play is a serious business

The four-week stage is also when your kitten begins to learn about social relationships, both with his mother and with his siblings. The great thing about kitten play from the owner's point of view is that it is such a joy to watch. The little ones totter about, clamber over each other, pounce from supposed hiding places, paw pat and grab at tails, both large and small, as a litter-mate or mum goes by.

The reality, of course, is that play is a necessary part of the growing process. It helps strengthen muscles, joints and ligaments, mature the senses and the nervous system, and expand the range of experiences that each kitten needs to fit him for the challenges that lie ahead.

Up, up and away

When he is five to six weeks of age your kitten should be able to start to control his eliminations and to move out of the nest when he needs to relieve himself. The toileting facilities that are available at this time have implications for future house training. If they're inappropriate or inadequate future owners can have real problems with their new pets house soiling, which is in sharp contrast to the normally fastidious behaviour of our domestic cats.

Your kitten's milk teeth will be erupting by now, making suckling less comfortable for the mother, so she will be making determined efforts to wean him. He will also be much more active and on the move in every way.

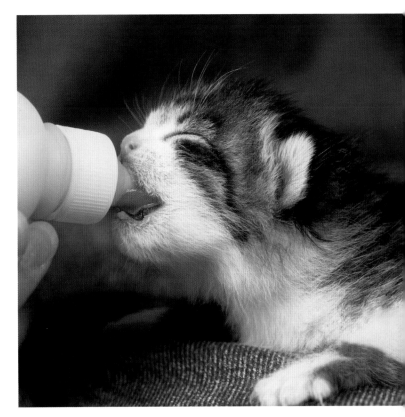

Left: From four weeks old, kittens will start to develop social relationships, playing and resting with their siblings.

Above: Hand rearing takes knowledge as well as dedication if kittens are to be well prepared for life in the future.

ONLY CAN BE LONELY
In the wild a single kitten is at a significant disadvantage compared to a kitten in a large litter because he has no one to practise with and more limited opportunities to learn through seeing what others do when his mother is away from the nest. Being a single kitten is not without problems for our pet cats, too. A lone kitten can find himself less able to cope well with frustration if he has been used to having all his mother's attention – not to mention that of devoted owners – during the early weeks. Hand rearing a singleton kitten needs particular care if he is to be successfully prepared to cope with the hard fact that once he's grown up, he won't always be able to get what he wants when he wants it.

Curiosity can kill the cat

Naturally, it makes sense for very young kittens to be nurtured and protected to the best of their mother's ability. However, this has to be balanced against their need to learn as much as they can about their world while they are still relatively safe. That's why kittens tend to be quite bold and outgoing in the early weeks.

BUYING A KITTEN
The optimal age to buy a kitten is between six and eight weeks. It's advisable not to buy a kitten that is under six weeks old. Ideally for maximum impact on your pet's behaviour, avoid kittens that are much older than eight weeks. Sometimes, especially with rescued kittens, owners don't have much choice. Then sensitive introductions can often make up for discrepencies, depending on the circumstances.

Learning to be cautious

If they continued to take everything head on, however, most cats would inevitably soon meet sticky ends, and to overcome this an interesting phenomenon occurs when kittens are six to eight weeks of age. It's at this time that kittens begin to show a defensive reaction to things they haven't previously encountered in a non-threatening way. This explains why the early weeks are so important and why we need to take care if we're responsible for producing happy, well-adjusted pets.

As we've seen (pages 88–9), gently introducing our kittens to a range of humans, other pets, domestic equipment and so on will help them to form a picture of a world against which they can later judge anything new they come across. If a new object, living thing or noise approximates to something they are already familiar with, the novel item will seem much less threatening than it might otherwise. The further away from their established template the new stressor looks and behaves, the greater the degree of fear they experience. Cats that have not had the right socialization and habituation experiences really struggle to fit in with any domestic environment, something that has repercussions for anyone who lives with them or cares for them in an amateur or professional capacity.

What's the best age to get your kitten?

Most owners won't have had their kitten from birth but will have acquired him from a breeder or a friend, and the question of what age you should take a kitten away from his mother and introduce him to a new home is hotly debated and causes significant differences of opinion. Difficulties can arise from the need to balance health risks, especially those posed by transmissible infections, with behavioural requirements.

Immature animals are much more vulnerable to illness than those whose immune systems are fully functional, which is why some breeders will not let their kittens go to homes before they are 12 weeks of age. The official bodies governing the breeding and registering of pedigree cats in many countries also stipulate this age, but this causes concern among behaviourists, who would prefer that kittens have the

chance to adjust to their permanent homes while they are still at their most adaptable. Behaviourally, the ideal age seems to be between six to eight weeks, as long as the kitten is fit, well and physically robust enough to cope with the move.

Health and behaviour are not actually entirely separate issues. Any animal that was not adequately prepared to deal with his eventual home will probably be stressed by everything he encounters there. If he's really unfortunate, because of limited or negative early experiences, the environment will be so difficult for him to adjust to that he will remain fearful his whole life, which could severely undermine his health. A number of behavioural problems – fear-based aggression towards people or other cats and over-grooming, for example – can be caused by a disparity between what cats were brought up to expect and the world they later inhabit. Not only do such behaviours indicate that they are unhappy, but they can have serious repercussions on their long-term health.

Above: *When they leave their mother and siblings young kittens lose everything that is familiar but by ensuring their management and facilities reflect what they are used to, we can ease the transition.*

Left: *By exploring a full range of situations at between six and eight weeks of age, cats can better cope with unusual situations, helping them to adjust to life in a new home.*

Re-homing a kitten

When you are choosing a kitten the best way to avoid behavioural problems later in his life is to consider carefully all we've already learned about a cat's development and to weigh this information against the range of factors that we know can affect his personality and adaptability. Only then can you really select your new kitten, but before then you need to decide where you are going to find your new pet.

Finding the cat for you

The first question to consider is how appropriate a kitten's background has been in producing the right pet for you. This question is, in fact, just as relevant if you are going to acquire an adult cat. Personal preference will always play a part in any such decision:

- Some people prefer pedigree cats.
- Some don't feel strongly about the type of cat but want a kitten to have the fun of watching him grow up.
- Some prospective owners always choose adult rescue cats, either because they don't want the tie of looking after a kitten or because they want to give a deserving cat a good home.

Sometimes, of course, you won't be able to answer all the questions on the following checklist because there's no, or only limited, information about the cat's background history. However, it's always worth trying to fill in as much as possible to help you decide if a particular cat, infant or adult, is the right one for you. Revealing areas that make a choice questionable doesn't always mean that a cat that someone has set their heart on is out of the question. Some of the gaping holes in a pet's behavioural experience that

CHECKLIST

- Are his mother's background, personality and circumstances likely to produce the cat for you?

- Is his father known? If so, are his background, personality and circumstances likely to produce the cat for you?

- If you can meet and try to interact with one or both of the parents, are they comfortable with you?

- What does the parent's or parents' reaction to you tell you about the suitability of their offspring for a life with you?

- Does the kitten you want interact well and confidently with his siblings? If the kitten is not confident with his siblings, ask yourself if you want an unconfident pet.

- How does he interact with you? Bear in mind that he'll probably be a little shy with a stranger, but you should be wary if he is overtly fearful or aggressive.

- Find out who cares for the kittens to identify any discrepancies between the people he has been encountering until now and those he will live with.

- If you identify deficiencies in socialization ask what steps have been taken to broaden the kittens' outlook – for example, are visitors asked to handle them or did they perhaps have CDs of different people and domestic sounds played to them from an early age?

- Is the kitten's accommodation suitable for a cat that is destined to become a household pet? For example, a kitten that has been bred and kept in a cage in a cattery might find it difficult to adjust to life in a family home.

you have identified can be overcome by diligent, patient and sensitive handling on your part.

If careful consideration of the points in the checklist identifies some slight discrepancies between your kitten's early experiences and what you think he needs to be the pet you really want – he didn't initially meet children, for instance – acquiring him young and gently broadening his horizons may make up for lost time. If the gaps seem daunting, it will probably pay you to think again, especially if his guardian cannot, or will not, let him come to you until he's past that critical socialization and habituation period.

Above: Choosing a kitten from a litter isn't easy, but it is a good opportunity to observe his characteristics and that of his mother, giving you an insight into his personality and suitability.

Left: No pet comes with a guarantee but choosing carefully and trying not to let your heart rule your head is likely to get you off to a good start.

Juvenile period

The phase between the end of the socialization period and sexual maturity – from the age of about eight weeks to between five and eight months (depending on breed) – is an exciting time for both the cat and his owner. It's during this period that the kitten begins to develop his own character and to become an individual.

Below: Social play is a feature of very early kittenhood but things get more serious towards the end of the socialization period and this is reflected in the focus of the kittens' attention.

Right: A mature, entire tomcat has a rounder face and a tendency to wander further from the home in search of a mate.

Things get more serious

A kitten's attention tends to switch its focus at the seven- or eight-week watershed. From being largely concentrated on his litter-mates and mother – her tail not infrequently being a much-prized plaything – the kitten becomes more interested in objects. Balls, strings, mice (real or toy) – anything, in fact, that will engage his attention – has to be poked, patted, prodded and chased if it can be made to move and chewed if it can be pinned down long enough.

For both kitten and owner this is an endlessly fascinating and entertaining time, but there is a serious purpose behind the fun. Although you have been diligently providing his food at regular intervals, the characteristics that his ancestors needed to survive still underlie your kitten's actions. He will be using every opportunity to develop the skills he needs to hunt, even

though he'll never have to fend for himself. You will notice him practising the typical stalk, chase, pounce, pat and 'kill' movements that we can see in any feline game. Most pets fail to string the sequence together effectively enough to catch food, but even so, all the elements present in the hunting process can be seen, although when cats play by themselves with objects, with each other or with their owners the predatory behaviour is generally demonstrated in a fairly piecemeal and haphazard fashion.

Sexual maturity

Without human intervention, the onset of this phase is the point at which cats are able to produce offspring themselves. The timing can be different in pedigree and non-pedigree felines, with some individuals reaching sexual maturity at

18–20 weeks of age, whereas others are not sexually mature until they are six or seven months old or even later. As the sex hormones begin to exert their effects, both sexes undergo significant physical changes, which have important behavioural consequences.

Male cats

Tomcats go through distinctive anatomical changes when they become sexually mature. If your cat is a male and you delay neutering him, you will notice his muscles developing under the influence of testosterone. He will also start developing the characteristic chubbier cheeks of male cats, and he is likely to be away from home for longer periods and venture further afield if he has access to outdoors.

The one thing you will be most unlikely to miss is the increased pungency of his urine, an odour that is rarely forgotten once it's been smelled. Unsurprisingly, this is one of the principal reasons for neutering males.

Female cats

The changes in the female are less pronounced than in tomcats until she starts to cycle. Queens are seasonally polyoestrous, which means that they have breeding seasons, brought on by day length. During these, female cats come 'on heat' (come into season or call) for two to four days, unless they are mated, when they stop cycling. There may be two, or sometimes three, breeding seasons a year, generally in spring, summer and possibly autumn. Cats are quite individual, however, so cycling can be variable and can be affected by breeders who, for example, keep their cats in artificial light to encourage cycles at particular times.

Mating and neutering

One of the most important decisions you will make about your cat, especially if you have a female, is whether to let her mate and have a litter or two or whether you will have the cat, male or female, neutered at the earliest opportunity. This is particularly important with male cats, who can cause owners problems if they are allowed to roam far and wide before they have been neutered.

Mating

If you have a female pedigree cat and want to breed from her, you should talk to your veterinarian about the optimum time to introduce her to a potential mate of the same breed. If you have a non-pedigree cat and simply let her out when she is ready to breed, she may mate with the first entire male cat she comes across.

Whether it happens in the controlled environment of a cattery or in a neighbour's back garden, copulation is a speedy, somewhat fraught process. The male mounts the queen, grasps her scruff in his mouth and triggers her into releasing an egg when he withdraws his penis with its backward pointing spines. This is a painful moment, and she generally yells and may bite him.

It usually pays to neuter

You're probably wondering what effects, if any, neutering or de-sexing, as it is also known, will have on your cat's behaviour.

Unless you have a pedigree and intend to breed under controlled conditions or are intent on having a litter with your non-pedigree cat – after taking your veterinarian's advice, of course – you will probably elect to neuter your pet.

The earlier the influence of the sex hormones is removed, the greater the physical, and to some extent at least the behavioural, differences will be. Many people neuter cats before the onset of puberty to remove the risk of sexually transmitted diseases and the potential for accidental injuries that seem to accompany the greater than normal exploration of both sexes in search of mating opportunities. Entire tomcats, in particular, appear to become involved in more road traffic accidents than their neutered counterparts. They certainly fight more, with all the attendant risks of disease and infection, and as a result generally become the classic picture of the battered old warrior at quite an early age.

Queens, too, can get worn out by repeated pregnancies and nursing of kittens, and many owners prefer to eliminate the unpleasant aspects of mating behaviour, such as spraying and caterwauling, and to spare their pets the obvious physical risks associated with the entire state.

Neutered cats of both sexes tend to convert the same number of calories to fat more readily after their operations, so you'll have to watch their weight or they will become more sluggish and inactive. On the plus side, you will iron out the periodic cycling behaviour of your queen, and your male is likely to retain his immature looks and be more youthfully docile than an entire tom. He will certainly smell less strongly.

The territorial instincts of neutered cats are also generally reduced, and territory may be less of an issue than in entire animals, where the male is always likely to be more driven to territorial expansion than the female, but even an entire female cat will vigorously defend the resources her potential young may need. In many ways de-sexing male and female cats can be said to allow them all the joys of adolescence without the risks and responsibilities of growing up. From our point of view, this state of neotony, as it is termed, means (as long as their breeding and socialization allow this) that we have affectionate, docile feline companions to share our lives and allow us to dote on them.

CASTRATION AND SPAYING
Tomcats are neutered by castration, the removal of the testicles. Some males have undescended testicles and require an abdominal operation to locate and remove them. For a female cat spaying involves an ovario-hysterectomy (the removal of the ovaries and uterus).

Ageing gracefully

Despite the un-neutered domestic cat's quite early interest in the opposite sex, he does not officially become an adult until he is 10–12 months old, and full physical maturity and the behavioural 'settling down' that marks social maturity won't really be reached until he is around 18–24 months of age. Neutered cats, as we have seen, reach a more 'subdued' physical maturity than their intact counterparts. Then, they soldier on for a good few years until they achieve the status of senior pet.

Elderly cats

Advances in nutrition and health care mean that there are now many more geriatric cats than previously. Ageing is a normal process, not a disease, but it does lead to a gradual and inevitable decline in the functioning of many of the body systems. As a result, the behaviour of elderly cats, those from eight to ten years onwards, can change, as their sight, hearing and sense of smell decline and they become less energetic and less mobile.

The good news is that we can do so much to ensure that your cat continues to enjoy a good quality of life. As he grows older you may need to make some adjustments to his management to make life easier for him. For instance, he may need low-level, comfortable resting places, whereas previously he used to prefer a high bed. Your cat may also become increasingly reluctant to go outside when it's cold and wet, and he may be unsettled or even intimidated by young cats that intrude into his territory. An easily accessible litter tray is essential at this time.

Watch out for any significant changes in his behaviour and make sure you take him for regular veterinary check-ups. The sooner that your vet can investigate warning signs, the more effective the treatment and support is likely to be. Many cats, of course, fall into the successful and gracefully ageing group, going on to live full, happy and very long lives. Once again, it's the combined effects of genetic inheritance, individuality and circumstances that tend to determine how your cat will cope with growing older.

THE OWNER'S VIEW

Looking in this way at all the important developmental stages that your cat will go through as his life progresses serves to remind us, as if we needed reminding, just how fascinating feline behaviour is and how many factors, intentional or otherwise, can affect your cat. It's also apparent that for us as owners knowing what to expect at any stage gives us the best possible chance of getting things right when it comes to caring for our cats, psychologically as well as physically, throughout what we hope will be a long life. Doing so will afford us the maximum possible pleasure as we watch our cat or cats grow and develop as the years pass.

Left: Spending more of their time sleeping in comfortable places, older cats are generally more subdued and settled.

Below: Senior pets are increasing in number and there is much more that can now be done to ensure they enjoy a good quality of life right up to the end.

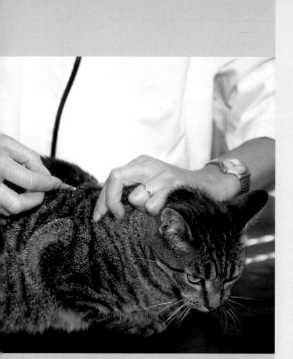

Senile dementia

It has recently been discovered that cats, like dogs and humans, can develop a form of senile dementia. In dogs the condition is called Cognitive Dysfunction Syndrome (CDS), and some behaviourists have suggested that the term should also be used for cats.

WHAT CAUSES THE CONDITION?

The signs of dementia may be mild or severe, and the progress of the disease is variable, with some cats rapidly deteriorating while others only slowly go downhill.

Our understanding of the disease is currently fairly limited, and we are only just beginning to learn about it and its similarities and differences to and from human Alzheimer's disease and CDS in dogs. It is, however, known that some of the changes seen during post mortems on the brains of affected cats are similar to those seen in human and canine sufferers. The behavioural signs, which are all there is to alert owners, are similar too.

Above: *Don't delay taking your elderly cat for a check up if you notice any changes in his behaviour. The earlier problems are detected the better.*

Right: *An elderly cat suffering from dementia may become withdrawn and lethargic, and you may notice that his eating and grooming habits also change.*

The signs of dementia shown by affected cats include:

• Disorientation
• Confusion
• Memory impairment
• Changes in social interactions: the cats can become unresponsive and withdrawn or the opposite, overly and unusually demanding of attention
• Loss of house training
• Excessive vocalization
• Night-time wakefulness combined with daytime lethargy
• Pacing and wandering aimlessly
• Altered appetite
• Altered self-hygiene and grooming behaviour

It is probable that this is a complicated condition and that a number of risk factors contribute to its development. For example, high blood pressure, something that is known in humans to be a contributory issue in dementia cases, is not uncommon in elderly cats, and it has been identified as one possible factor that may be implicated. Free radicals, reactive groups of atoms, which are known to be responsible for some of the changes involved in the aging process, are also likely to play a part in the feline syndrome.

HOW WIDESPREAD IS THE CONDITION?

It is difficult to know how many cats are actually affected by dementia because some owners may not notice the signs, especially if their pet is only mildly affected. Other owners, of course, will realize that something is going wrong but put it down to 'normal' ageing. Even your veterinarian may have difficulty diagnosing the condition as the changes in your cat can be ascribed to some other age-related medical problems with similar symptoms.

HOW IS IT DIAGNOSED?

This is not a condition for which a test can prove or disprove that an individual pet is affected. The diagnosis depends on eliminating all other possible diseases that could be causing the signs by identifying and effectively treating the symptoms. Then, the behavioural signs need to be examined in depth to make sure that a more straightforward behavioural problem is not responsible for the changes that the owner has noticed in the way their cat interacts with them and his environment. It can be complicated, take time to sort out the evidence and make an ultimate diagnosis, and it will probably require the involvement of a qualified feline behaviourist.

IS THERE A TREATMENT?

Sadly, there is no specific remedy for feline dementia at present, but supportive treatments are available that can help delay the condition's progress and reverse some of the clinical signs. The response to diets specially enriched with antioxidants, drugs that increase the blood flow to the brain or that have a neuroprotective action is variable, but these treatments can be helpful in some of the pets identified as suffering from the disease.

Some owners may not persist with their pet, especially if he has become very difficult to live with or appears to be suffering. However, if your cat is elderly, don't worry. Just enjoy his company as usual, go to your veterinarian if you notice anything amiss, and make sure you attend regular senior pet check-ups which should pick up conditions that don't cause overt signs in the early stages.

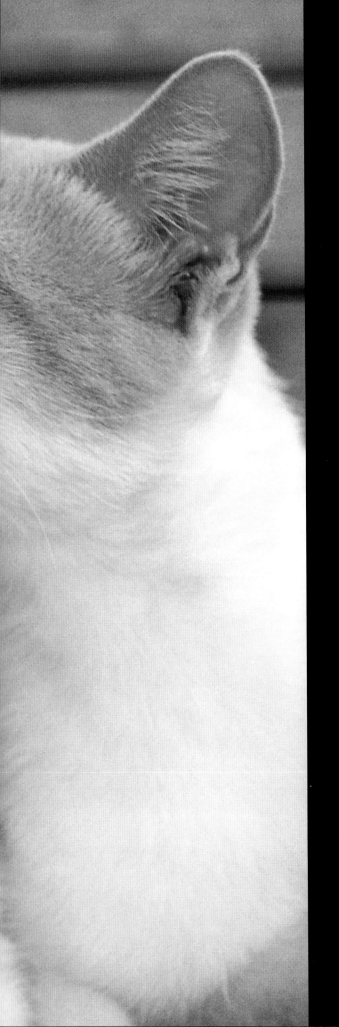

LIFESTYLE ISSUES

The pressures of the modern world and changing population demographics are affecting the lives of cats and their owners alike. Feline household members are much more part of the family than they used to be in the past, and concerns for their safety and our increased high-rise living have led more people to decide to keep their cats permanently indoors, previously a rare feline lifestyle. In addition, the increased popularity of the cat has contributed, among other factors, to a rapid increase in the number of homes containing more than one feline companion. There are risks and benefits associated with any lifestyle, and when you are deciding what's best for your cat it pays to be fully aware of the pros and cons associated with each possible option before making your choice.

Indoor cats and multi-cat homes

Veterinarians and behaviourists are increasingly concerned about the stresses that underlie many of the problem behaviours and some of the medical conditions for which pet owners seek their help. All too often these result directly from the lifestyles imposed on affected cats – albeit with the best of intentions – by their owners.

Lifestyle problems

It is known that Feline Lower Urinary Tract Disease (FLUTD; see pages 128–9) and obesity (see pages 124–5) are linked to cats' lifestyles. In addition, the causes of some of the common behavioural problems that all too frequently put a cat on a collision course with its owners, and at the same time potentially undermine a treasured pet's quality of life and emotional welfare, are also associated with lifestyle. These include:

- Fear
- Anxiety
- Frustration
- Motivational conflict
- Boredom
- Indolence

That these behaviours are more frequently encountered in multi-cat homes or those where a singleton or feline group has no access to the outside world, should come as no great surprise now that you have looked at the evolution of the cat and all the important aspects of their natural behaviour.

Above: *A catflap gives your cat the choice of coming and going, and some models can be locked to prevent unwanted visitors gaining access.*

Left: *Circumstances are likely to dictate whether your cat has an indoor only or free ranging lifestyle but try to weigh all the pros and cons before deciding which it is to be.*

Behaviourists are now talking about 'environmental enrichment', a concept first identified as being helpful in alleviating the behavioural abnormalities that developed in captive exotic animals, and demonstrating that it can be enormously useful when applied to our cats. Environmental enrichment is often crucially important in resolving problems, but obviously prevention is always better than cure. An added bonus of the measures that have been designed to keep indoor cats happy is they involve owners and pets having fun together.

It can be done
Both indoor lifestyles and multi-cat homes can be made to work succesfully – given an appropriate choice of cats – if sensitivity and effort, generally mixed with a good deal of compromise, are invested by owners. Life is never an entirely risk-free business, but if you are forced by circumstances to keep your cat indoors all the time or have decided to do so on grounds of his safety, it pays to make sure you've really thought things through and considered both the pros and cons of indoor life.

THE PROS AND CONS OF AN INDOOR LIFE
The benefits include:
- A reduced risk of accidental injury from road traffic, drowning, tumbles from trees, fences and the like.
- A reduced risk of acquiring infectious diseases.
- Reduction of the stress associated with peer pressure if the local feline population is high.

The disadvantages include:
- Accidents still happen at home: slips and spills off furniture and the stairs; incidents with the washer and tumble dryer; poisoning from plants and toxic substances; burns and scalds.
- A lack of street wisdom and good sense if your cat is accidentally lost.
- The stress caused by the incursion into their territory by other cats, which may be seen through the window or smelled when doors and windows are opened or when items that smell of other cats are introduced into the home.

THE PROS AND CONS OF AN OUTDOOR LIFE
The benefits include:
- More space and better facilities to indulge all your cat's natural needs.
- A greater sense of control over his life, which is what all cats want.
- An increased ability to escape from intolerable pressures, fear or anxieties associated with the home and/or its residents, whether two- or four-legged.

The disadvantages include:
- Modern, minimalist garden design often robs outdoor spaces of the facilities that allow cats to enjoy themselves: there may be no mature trees, few if any shrubs to hide behind and no suitable latrine areas.
- Other cats can enter the resident's core area via the catflap if there is one or through open doors or windows.
- Outdoors may be just as pressurized as indoors, and your cat's ability to indulge his needs may be limited by peer pressure from a high local feline population.

How your cat sees his home

Before you do anything, it's important to interpret your cat's home through his eyes, bearing in mind all cats' natural behaviour and your own cat's personality, or, if your new pet has yet to arrive, what you can glean from knowledge of his breed, his individual CV and your initial contact with him.

Back to basics

Remember the basic requirements for any cat to feel comfortable and in control of his environment, bear in mind that cats need to be able to indulge in such activities as exploring, 'hunting', sleeping, eliminating in an appropriate location and so on.

Territory is just as important for indoor cats as it is for their cousins that have free access to outdoors. It's immediately clear that normal territorial divisions are telescoped for indoor cats, whose ability to range is artificially curtailed. Unless they live in a mansion, their available space is likely to be much smaller than their natural inclinations would prefer,

especially, of course, when they share with a number of people, other cats and different types of pets or are restricted to limited parts of the home.

It's equally obvious, therefore, that anything that affects the integrity – physically, visually and in scent or noise terms – of their territory is going to have a significant emotional impact on any cat kept indoors. A good general rule is that the richer the environment from the feline perspective and the less disruption there is, the happier the cat will be.

What your cat's environment must do

If an indoor life is going to work for your cat your home must provide him with:

- A sense of security: his home must be predictable and non-stressful.
- A sense of control: the ability to make his own decisions is as important for keeping a cat on an even keel as it is for his owner.
- Complexity and interest, as long as it is not frightening.
- Cat-friendly novelty to satisfy the needs of your cat's active mind and body.
- Social contact of your cat's choice not anyone else's: no one should impose attention on him when he doesn't care

STAYING IN CONTROL
When they are introduced to a new environment cats, especially if they're timid or a bit nonplussed by circumstances, usually prefer to go to 'non-cat' people because cat lovers are nearly always too keen to make friends as quickly as possible. This inadvertent pressure generally means that cats head straight for the least willing lap and sit happily there, untouched and unfussed, for an insultingly long time. The cat is in control and he knows it.

for it or if he's wary because of limited socialization experiences or negative associations through previous unfortunate incidents.

Outdoor pens

Some people decide that constructing an outdoor pen will be the ideal way to give their indoor cat an opportunity for a change of scene and some fresh air. If the cat can decide when he makes his outdoor forays – through a catflap or adjacent open window, say – this can be a good solution for the cat. Sadly though, it's too often the owner who determines the cat's timetable – so much for the cat's need for control.

Unfortunately, outdoor cages are also frequently inadequately furnished, so the confined cat is exposed to the view of other felines but does not have the means of hiding or escape, which is extremely intimidating for the penned cat. The cat may also be stressed by the scent of neighbouring cats that regard the site of the pen as part of their territory because they're free to mark it as such, but the actual resident can do nothing to stake his claim. In fact, he may even be regarded as the intruder, and every time he comes (or is forced) out he will be confronted by clear scent messages that he shouldn't be there. That is not a recipe for feline happiness.

Harnesses and leads pose the same types of problem and should similarly be used with care.

ENRICHING THE ENVIRONMENT
Ensuring your cat's territory provides plenty of opportunities for him to exercise all his natural behaviours, such as climbing, exploring, 'hanging out' and hiding, need not be costly. Thoughtful planning and a little effort can transform most homes into satisfying feline environments. When cats are free to go in and out owners often assume they have no part to play in their activities. What a mistake. A barren outdoor space is intimidating and a recipe for problem behaviour. Applying the same principles outdoors as indoors can easily transform a garden into a stimulating feline playground.

Above: At home and outside using 3D space to create elevated platforms, walkways, shelves and enclosed hiding places helps owners provide a truly feline-friendly environment.

Left: Using a lead to 'walk' your cat may cause him distress as he will feel vulnerable and lack control in an unfamiliar setting.

Selective breeding has created a range of pedigree cats that display certain characteristics and specific personality traits. Other factors also influence each pet's behaviour, but it helps prospective owners to know what tendencies their favoured breed will inherit to ensure they'll enjoy their cat's company and be able to adequately cater for all his needs. This information should give you an insight into some of the most popular cat breeds.

Breed personalities

ABYSSINIAN
Sociable with people, these intelligent, playful adventurers make amusing companions, who enjoy learning tricks. They communicate with their owners by using voices that are less raucous than other breeds, but because they are quite independent they're not necessarily good candidates for multi-cat homes.

BENGAL
Beautiful cats that resulted from crossing the Asian Leopard, a wild feline, and Domestic Short Hair cats, the three generations after the original mating were not temperamentally predisposed to make good pets. However, the Bengals now available, provided they're adequately socialized, are inquisitive, confident, friendly and people orientated. Highly intelligent, they need company and plenty to occupy their time and their minds.

BIRMAN
Sweet tempered, sensitive and playful throughout their lives, Birmans are great lap cats that become very attached to owners and can be stressed if left alone a lot.

BRITISH SHORT HAIR
These friendly, placid cats have a tendency to laziness, love food and are not especially active, so they can put on weight. Their steady temperaments and enjoyment of human company, without a strong need for it, make them easy attractive pets.

BURMESE
Energetic, active, curious and easily bored, these intelligent cats make loving, sociable pets with a tendency to attention seeking, so they cannot cope with being under stimulated or left 'home alone' for long periods.

CORNISH AND DEVON REX
These are real people cats. Home loving, affectionate companions they are by no means dim or indolent, and being curious and playful need the company of others, two- or four-legged.

MAINE COON
Hardy and independent, these large cats need space and outlets for their intelligence. They are affectionate and sociable with owners but not really lap cats, although they enjoy learning tricks and are a good choice for people who like feline companions with somewhat dog-like qualities!

OCICAT
Another breed with dog-like attachment to owners, these sociable cats are bright, active and vocal. In need of

constant stimulation and company, Ocicats don't fare well in small homes and if left alone for long periods.

PERSIAN

For owners with the patience to keep their long fine coats in order, this is an affectionate, companionable and easy going breed, at home inside as well as out, although they are renown for being somewhat clumsy as well as playful.

RAGDOLL

These cats are known for their gentle and tolerant natures, although this should never be taken for granted, despite their willingness to put up with cuddling and fairly intrusive handling. Intelligent, with an aptitude for training, they are thought to require less exercise and space than other breeds and to be relatively uninterested in hunting.

RUSSIAN BLUE

Gentle and quiet, this breed can be shy with strangers, and generally prefers a stable territory with a predicable routine, although they are intelligent cats and make good companions.

SIAMESE

Not companions for those unprepared to be harangued by loud demanding voices! These active, intelligent, sociable cats need constant stimulation and company, so attention seeking can become a problem but they're fun to train and will never be boring.

TURKISH VAN

Intelligent, friendly cats, renowned for their love of water. Good companions for owners, many Turkish vans enjoy training and learning tricks such as retrieving games.

Right: *The curious and lively Burmese make loving pets that enjoy human company.*

Left: *People often fall for the looks of a particular pedigree breed but not checking out its personality profile as well can lead to problems later.*

Ideal homes

Providing your indoor cat with plenty of opportunities to exercise as he would in the wild, is one of the best ways there is of avoiding potential behavioural problems, but your cat's other needs, including his inbuilt requirement to identify and mark his territory, should not be overlooked.

Resting and sleeping

Your cat's ancestors didn't want to hang around long in one place advertising their presence to nearby predators, and frequently moving from one favoured sleeping spot to another also helped to control external parasites (fleas and ticks). These same tactics probably underlie your cat's tendency to 'fall in love' with a particular place, being seemingly glued to it for a couple of weeks, then never returning. Moreover, when you remember the feline need for control, it's no surprise to learn that each cat needs a choice of beds, a variety of styles to test preferences and in a range of different locations to suit the mood of the moment. When it comes to feline resting, sleeping and hiding places every cat needs high-level, low-level and floor-level options.

- Leave airing cupboard or wardrobe doors open, as long as you don't mind crumpled, hairy clothes and linen, to provide an opportunity for exploring and a comfy bed.
- Clear cases and storage boxes from under beds and leave the bedcover or some bedclothes hanging down to make a comforting, dark refuge.
- Decluttering the tops of furniture, such as wardrobes, chests of drawers and bookshelves, quickly provides hiding and observation posts for resident felines.
- Make some cardboard box kennels by turning boxes on their side and place them on top of furniture, on bookshelves, along corridors and hallways, giving some of them a newspaper curtain by sticking a sheet to the top so that it hangs down over the opening to make an ideal refuge for a timid pet.
- Place a favourite sweater in a sunny spot or a fleecy blanket by a fireside or heater.
- Leave paper carrier bags (without handles) on the floor where they can be adopted by cats as a temporary shelter.

What about marking?

Inappropriate indoor marking is usually highly appropriate in feline terms when the affected locations are related to natural cat behaviour. The sofa will be stropped if it's near the doorway, for example, where there is no suitable 'legitimate' scratching material. Curtains serve well for stropping if the open window brings in another cat's scent, impelling the resident to satisfy his need for security by obliterating it with his own.

It's important, therefore, to provide a number of scratching posts or other materials – as long as you choose something that enables your cat to leave visual marks – in suitable locations. Protect good furniture that is in 'vulnerable' positions by draping old blankets over it, and in a small house sticking carpet or sisal behind entrance doors or on nearby walls or wrapping it round stair posts can avoid your having to sacrifice valuable floor space as well as protecting doorframes. And, don't forget that your cat may be one that likes to mark horizontally, so offer him a choice of vertical and flat scratching posts and pads.

CLEANING REGIME
A clean litter tray is an essential, but do not use strong disinfectants or artificial odours to disinfect the tray – we might like the fragrance of pine, but cats do not. Regularly scoop out and dispose of soiled areas and make sure that excreta does not build up. Replace all the litter at least once a week.

Avoiding too thorough cleaning that removes all the reassuring odours your cat has left just at his height by bunting and rubbing, can not only make a huge difference to your cat's emotional wellbeing but will also protect your furnishings from damage by stropping.

Eating and drinking

Remember that eating and drinking are separate activities in your cat's world, so divide up the facilities, experiment and make full use of the entertainment value offered by both activities. Details are given in the special spreads on pages 44–5 and 126–7.

Toileting facilities

This is an area where owners of indoor-only cats often come to grief, and it's a subject that frequently leads to stress for the cat and subsequent inappropriate behaviour that upsets the harmony of the relationship. It's also one where there is no one-size-fits-all solution.

Types of litter were discussed on pages 64–5, but the choice and positioning of the litter tray are also crucial. An enclosed litter tray has the advantages that it is private and the litter is contained so that it makes less mess. However, enclosed trays have the disadvantages that fumes from excreta build up, making it unpleasantly smelly from the cat's point of view, some cats don't like entering a dark tunnel and others feel uncomfortably confined. An open tray, while rarely smelly, has the major disadvantage for your cat that it is not private.

When you are positioning the tray remember to place it somewhere private and preferably near the edge of the cat's territory so that it is easy and not intimidating to reach.

Left: Providing sufficient, satisfactory and suitably located scratching posts is the best way to protect your home from your cat's stropping.

Far left: Floor-level hiding places under furniture or in boxes provide different beds for your cat's instinctive need to change resting places.

Playing and socializing

Boredom and frustration are the two great enemies of cats, especially those kept indoors. Fortunately, little effort or expense is needed to create interesting feline playgrounds – just as human infants invariably find the box an expensive present came in infinitely more engaging than the toy itself, cats are frequently absorbed by playthings they discover for themselves or that their owners construct from throw-away items.

Left: Television and videos can also entertain cats. Looking to their natural behaviour helps us to find the topics and pictures that are most likely to absorb them.

Right: Provide your pet with fresh catnip in the garden and you could have instant entertainment as he rolls in the flower beds in apparent ecstasy.

To play or not to play

Many commercial cat toys are designed to attract owners, and they have little value for pets. Cats play with prey, so it's not surprising that they enjoy poking, batting, chasing and pouncing on small, light, swiftly moving objects. Anything that could, safely, substitute for a mouse can easily become a favourite plaything, including corks from wine bottles, screws of tissue paper, scraps of fur fabric and pieces of cardboard tube.

One important aspect of play is that it provides an outlet for predatory behaviour and all the stages of the hunting sequence. Your cat must be able to tear to pieces anything he's managed to capture – as long as it's safe – just as he would if he were catching his own dinner. Dispensing his food in imaginative ways is useful and fun.

Another benefit of play is the opportunities it offers for bonding and social interaction, something indoor cats also need. Throwing toys or dangling rods with feathers on a line provide ideal introductions between cats and unfamiliar people. These games leave your cat in control, and he can ignore both toy and human or engage with both sufficiently far away to maintain a comfortable flight distance if he's disposed to do so. If your cat is timid, or if the person is anxious, this safe, positive method can cement relationships as well as increasing mental and physical activity for a captive pet. It's easy to maintain novelty, another essential, by rotating the available toys and examining everything that comes along for its potential role as feline entertainment.

Borrowed landscapes

Don't forget the value of outdoors in keeping your indoor pet's brain ticking over. Cats need access to daylight, and sitting on windowsills watching the world, natural and manmade, go by can be a stimulating occupation. Hanging mobiles, glitter balls or even bird feeders outside will provide a constantly changing focus for your cat's attention. He may sometimes 'chatter' in anticipation as he watches the birds swooping and diving nearby. It's important to remember that windows must be kept closed or protected by grills so that he can't fall out, and you should try to make sure that nothing he sees causes him anxiety.

CATNIP
Your cat may be thrilled with catnip (*Nepeta cataria*) or totally indifferent. If it's the latter, there's nothing wrong with him. He may be too young – it's a liking that doesn't develop until sexual maturity – or he may just not be genetically programmed that way. The tendency to be 'turned on', so that contact with the plant itself or toys containing it induces even in neutered cats the rolling and rubbing associated with sexual activity, is inherited. The scent of the leaves often induces the Flehmen response (see page 17), but it's still not known for certain exactly what it does to our cats, although an hallucinogenic state has been suggested.

Multi-cat homes

Problem behaviour can occur when there is just one cat, but sadly the incidence of these problems increases in multi-cat homes. Some multi-cat households are genuinely harmonious. However, unrecognized feline tension may bubble beneath the surface or periodic explosions may make it obvious that your cats are not happy. There are several reasons why homes containing more than one cat are often a recipe for feline stress, no matter how caring the owners are, and they mostly relate back to normal cat behaviour.

Inappropriate choice of individuals

We don't necessarily like living in close proximity to a person that someone else has chosen as our companion, and we like it even less when there are several of them. Yet we expect cats to do just this. Groups of cats are often composed of unrelated adults, which have been brought together on the whim of their owners. Some may be sociable and enjoy close contact with other cats. Some, by virtue of their temperament and experience, will be disinclined to do so but will tolerate the situation. Others, however, will be overtly hostile, and these cats are frequently (and wrongly) labelled as dominant or bullies.

Unrealistic expectations of the cats

If we relate most multi-cat homes to natural circumstances, the inescapable fact emerges that in nature cats control the composition of their group. In a multi-cat home they have no choice and can exercise no control over their companions. Frequently, therefore, a household of cats actually consists of a number of different feline social groups, sometimes as many as there are cats in the home. Natural inclination would lead these individuals to:

• Avoid each other completely
• Lead solitary lives based around their individual territories and the facilities they contain

• Use normal feline communication methods to keep as much space as possible between them

Neutering tends to make cats less aggressive towards other groups, which obviously helps to some degree, but unfortunately, we all too often unwittingly impose unfair expectations on our cats because we have so little regard for the natural basis of their behaviour, something cats are powerless to change.

Hasty or insensitive introduction procedures

Some cats might get on better if they had been given longer to get to know each other.

Insufficient space

To compound the stress of living cheek by jowl with one or more cats, the homes that contain several cats are often not particularly large. The situation is made even worse when the cats are denied the one possible means of diffusing tension by increasing space between them because they have no access to outdoors or elevated hiding places and escape routes. Ingenious use of shelves, platforms, walkways and furniture can improve the environment and reduce stress in multi-cat homes.

Lack of facilities

Owners of several cats frequently regard a lack of overt hostilities as evidence of harmony. For instance, they cite the fact that their cats come together to eat as an indication that they enjoy each other's company, overlooking the fact that their pets usually eat in relays, each waiting until the other has finished before they approach the one food bowl – so much for the feline desire for choice. If hunger forces them together at the feeding station a spat invariably develops.

Remembering that cats generally only resort to fighting as a strategy when they are very stressed will put quite a different interpretation on such circumstances. How would we feel if the roles were reversed? This isn't anthropomorphism. It's understanding how stressful life can be for any species that has to live in conditions that are not appropriate to its natural needs.

Inappropriate location of facilities

The positioning of facilities in a multi-cat household can be as much of an issue as their quantity and quality.

External feline pressure

Where local cat populations are high, outside stress can spill over into homes, creating – or exacerbating – interior tensions, even where pets are kept indoors and only see, smell and hear neighbouring felines.

Left: Providing separate facilities, such as feeding and drinking bowls, will help to avoid tension at mealtimes.

Below: Multi-cat homes can work but owner expectations must be realistic.

Left: Sibling kittens are a good choice for harmony and as they mature they may groom each other and play together happily.

Right: Introducing a kitten to the household with a resident older cat should be a slow process that is closely supervised and controlled.

Multi-cat harmony

No matter how hard we try, there's never any guarantee that a multi-cat home will be happy and harmonious. However, by understanding the basis of your cats' behaviour, by respecting their individual differences, by appropriately choosing who will live together and by providing the right physical and social conditions, you can certainly make success more likely.

Choose cats with care

Undoubtedly the best combination of cats for starting a multi-cat home is two sibling kittens. It used to be thought that it was better to get different sexes, but now it seems that brothers can live quite amicably when they are neutered early on. Females tend to be more territorial, although, as ever, individuality comes into play. If siblings are not available, you could try introducing unrelated kittens of the same age.

As they mature your cats may still be happy to groom each other and to share food bowls, beds and their owner's

attention, but some cats, related or not, become more independent as they grow older. Your management regime may need to change as time goes by in line with their altered style of interaction.

If you are thinking about getting a second adult cat to live with you, it's best to choose a younger one of the opposite sex, but do bear the other important issues in mind, such as those listed on the opposite page. Always ask yourself if it's fair to your resident cat to enlarge the feline component of your home. He may prefer it if you let him remain a singleton.

Have realistic expectations of your cats

If you are creating a multi-cat home from unrelated adults it's essential to:

- Be realistic about the number of cats that your environment, interior and exterior, can reasonably accommodate, and if this doesn't accord with your desires you should compromise – cats can't.
- Choose cats that are predisposed to have a good chance of getting on together. Many cats suffer because people attempt the impossible.
- Create a suitable practical set-up in your household to cater for them all.
- Treat your cats as individual social groups, providing separate territories with a full set of all the necessary facilities in each area.
- Introduce them with care and patience. Setting arbitrary timetables and deadlines is a recipe for disaster.

Having somewhere to hide is especially important if you are introducing one cat to an existing feline group or two new cats into your home, and in these circumstances placing everything that the cats require in appropriate locations is more important than ever.

Finally, you must accept that you may love them equally, but your cats may never feel the same way about each other.

Introductions

Insensitive attitudes such as 'let them get on with it' are foolish and downright unethical. Allow each cat to settle individually, then gradually, carefully monitoring their reactions for any signs of anxiety, use scent exchange to create positive associations and a communal odour.

When the time is right, keep face-to-face contact minimal and very brief. It's essential that you build up slowly to your cats spending longer supervised periods together.

Never take chances and leave your pets alone together unless, and until, they are really well adjusted to each other.

AFTERWARDS

Even if all goes well, remember the long-term needs of your cats. Never force them to share anything when they really need separate areas of activity. Anticipate and plan for potentially stressful events that may upset their established harmony, such as veterinary trips, building work, visitors or changes in your social group – a new partner or the arrival of your first baby. After all, both you and your cats have a lot to lose if everything goes awry, all because of a lack of sensitivity and care.

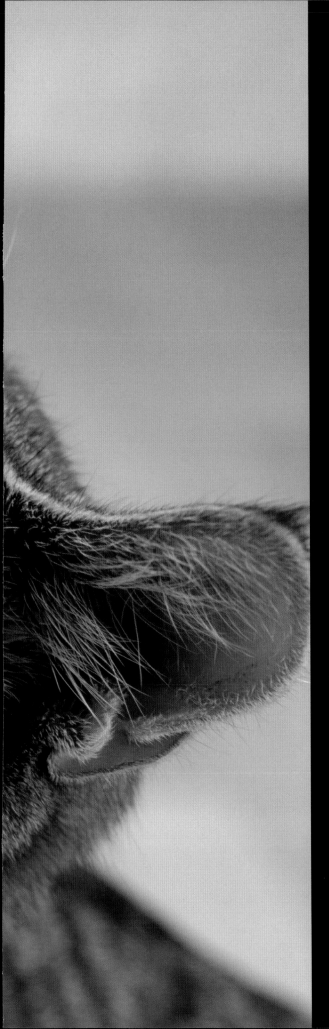

HEALTH AND SICKNESS

Keeping your cat happy means keeping him healthy. You can play your part in helping him maintain peak condition, no matter what his age, by ensuring that he has a well-balanced diet; adequate physical exercise; the right environment to keep his mind active; and regular health checks, vaccinations and preventative treatments to control internal and external parasites, intestinal worms, fleas and ticks. Good health and normal behaviour go hand in hand, and when one is out of balance the other is invariably negatively affected. Good nutrition and health care are about keeping your cat fit and well, but keeping him emotionally well balanced and happy are just as important.

Monitoring health

Being familiar with your cat's normal behaviour patterns and his usual appearance is essential. Knowing, for example, what he usually eats and drinks, how he looks and what he does means that you are unlikely to miss changes that indicate something is amiss.

Above: *This healthy bright-eyed cat is alert and agile. When you are familiar with your cat's normal appearance and behaviour you are more likely to spot signs that something is amiss.*

Right: *An unhealthy cat will exhibit physical signs of ill health, such as watery eyes and matted fur, and should be examined by the vet.*

However, don't be put off seeking advice if you know something's wrong but just can't put your finger on it. When you are really familiar with your cat, you might identify suspicious changes before there's any obvious sign. The sooner your veterinarian gets involved, the easier most conditions are to treat. It's always better to be safe than sorry.

Things can go wrong

Sadly, pathological changes can develop in any of a cat's cells, tissues, organs or major systems. Many diseases or specific problems can be seen at any life stage, although your cat will be more susceptible to some conditions at different times. For example, developmental abnormalities are most likely to show up in the early weeks or months of his life, whereas once he reaches his senior years he will have an increased risk of developing a larger range of age-related medical conditions.

Help is at hand

Fortunately, veterinary medicine and surgery can now do more to help than ever before, and there is a range of supportive nutritional care and complementary therapies. There is also increasing recognition of the importance of behavioural medicine when it comes to your cat's care. This discipline has the potential to work alongside medical and surgical interventions to help obtain the best results for your pet. Its value as part of a package of care for a number of conditions, including obesity, Feline Lower Urinary Tract Disease (FLUTD) and compulsive disorders, is now well established.

Moreover, it's not uncommon for disturbing behavioural changes to exacerbate, or develop as a result of, medical problems, and sadly, problem behaviour is a major reason for people giving up their cats or even having them put down.

The important role that behaviour counselling can play in restoring the quality of life of affected cats, and in repairing strained relationships with owners that are the consequence of behaviour problems, is increasingly recognized. And it pays cat owners to ensure they consult a specifically trained feline behaviourist when they need help with their cat's behaviour.

YOUR CAT IS WELL IF:
- His eyes are bright, with no redness, discharge or signs of swelling
- His nose is moist and clean
- His coat is glossy and his fur smooth, with no bald patches or signs of hair loss
- His appetite is normal – that is, he's not off food or eating more than normal
- His thirst is also normal – that is, he's drinking no more or less than usual
- His weight is stable – no changes up or down – and there are no alterations in his body shape
- He is alert and active (when he isn't sleeping) and has a spring in his step and no sign of stiffness, swelling or lameness

TAKE YOUR CAT TO THE VETERINARIAN IF:
- His eyes are dull, red, have swollen lids or a watery or messy discharge
- His nose is dry, crusty or running
- His coat loses its shine or is matted, scurfy or falling out in patches
- His skin is scabby, red or sore
- His appetite decreases, or increases dramatically, especially if this is combined with other signs
- His thirst increases, or he changes what he likes to drink
- He is lethargic, hides away, sleeps all day or loses interest in his usual activities
- He dribbles or eats on one side or claws at his mouth
- He reacts painfully if you touch him
- He coughs, sneezes or vomits
- He has laboured breathing, diarrhoea or constipation or difficulty passing urine
- He seems confused or disorientated or if he loses his balance, collapses or convulses

OR IF YOU:
- Notice a swelling or limp, stiffness, or a wound or bleeding
- See any subtle or inexplicable change in your pet's normal behaviour

Obesity as a behavioural issue

No matter what stage in life your cat has reached, good nutrition is essential for optimal health. Every cat has his own preferences for some food items and is less keen on others, and you'll no doubt get pleasure from indulging him. However, pandering too much to our pets' whims can be the type of kindness that kills.

REQUIREMENTS VARY
That a good diet is essential for physical fitness is something we all know. What you may not realize is that poor nutrition adversely affects learning and memory. If kittens and young cats don't get the right balance of all the essential nutrients needed during their developmental phases they may never be as behaviourally competent as they could have been. At the other end of the scale, older cats can lose their mental abilities if they don't receive the right diet for their life stage.

Special prescription diets can play a crucial role in maintaining an individual cat's overall health and returning his behaviour to normal. Your veterinarian is always the best source of advice about correctly feeding your cat, whatever his age or condition.

THE OBESITY EPIDEMIC
Just as with humans, there's increasing concern about the levels of obesity in our pet cat population. The health risks facing overweight cats are similar to those facing overweight humans, and the reasons for the problems are identical: too many calories and too little exercise. Changing lifestyles are as much to blame for the feline as for the human problem, and increased affluence, the greater variety on

supermarket shelves, the connection between food and expressing affection and the stresses of modern living, all play a part.

WHY IT HAPPENS
Cats have poor detoxification mechanisms, which can't deal well with spoiled food, and their taste systems are designed to detect decay rather than to pick and choose from the menu. In addition, prey populations in any area will be similar. Therefore, when cats have to hunt and catch their own dinners they have little choice over what they consume.

This is not the case when they come to a loving owner. We enjoy providing a range of flavours – it's how we show our love, but it's also why so many owners misinterpret their cat's desires when he rubs round their legs or chirrups a greeting while they are in the kitchen. 'He must be hungry,' we think. So out comes food, when all the cat really wanted was a little attention and some fun.

In addition, if he doesn't eat what we put down, we think it must be stale or that he doesn't like the flavour. So we promptly replace it with something new and tempting. At the same time, the meals we provide are invariably too

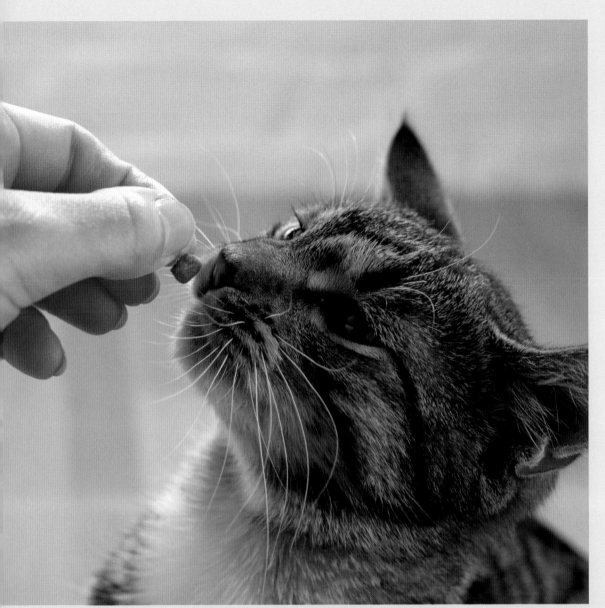

Left: Owners have a vital role to play in keeping their cats healthy, slim and happy, keeping treats to a minimum.

Far left: Obesity is increasing in our cat population and is detrimental to their health, happiness and life expectancy.

rich and too large because we can't bear the small quantities that the manufacturers recommend.

Another trap that owners fall into is that of petting and playing with cats after they've eaten as a reward for a 'nice clean plate'. Cats quickly learn that to get us to entertain them, they have to eat ... and eat they do.

Evidence now shows that other aspects of this problem are:

- Some cats 'feed for a famine' if a lot of food is available, regardless of whether they need or even really want the food.

- Highly palatable, tasty food overwhelms the normal mechanisms that tell cats they've had enough, thus encouraging them to carry on eating, like some owners with a box of chocolates.
- Other cats, like people, 'comfort eat', because the release of endorphins (naturally occurring opiates) that is associated with eating leads stressed cats to keep picking at food in an attempt to reduce their anxiety levels.
- While they are in high-stress situations, such as multi-cat homes, bolder individuals sometimes make mealtimes a source of anxiety for less confident cats, which tend to overeat when they can.

HEALTH RISKS OF OBESITY
Among the health risks associated with feline obesity are:

- Lethargy, indolence and reduced exercise tolerance
- Cardio-vascular problems
- Diabetes
- High blood pressure
- FLUTD (see pages 128–9)
- Osteoarthritis
- Reduced quality of life

Overcoming obesity

In order to overcome the problem of obesity in our cats we need to address the common lack of awareness of normal feline feeding patterns. We should also stop equating mealtimes with socializing: this is true for humans and for dogs, as pack hunters, but not our solitary hunting cats.

WHERE TO FROM HERE?

Cats naturally 'snack' on several small, mouse-sized meals every day, for which they work hard. Estimates suggest that in the wild between six and eight hours a day is spent hunting and that during this time between 100 and 150 attempts at a kill are made, but with a success rate of only about 10 per cent, resulting in 10–30 meals a day. Although the feline diet is calorie rich, the process of stalking, hunting and killing involves expending a lot of energy for not a huge return.

The more we can simulate the cats' natural feeding pattern, the healthier our cats will be. In addition, we really must address such issues as anxiety and tension, whatever it's source.

THE TREATMENT PLAN

Before you make any changes ask your veterinarian's advice about the best food for your cat. Then stick to one type of a balanced, all-round diet. Dry foods are useful because they don't become unappetizing if they are left down, but they should be topped up a couple of times daily, because the oils do evaporate.

Don't misinterpret your cat's approaches as demands for food.

If you're not sure what your cat wants try playing, petting, grooming or just being close at hand. If this works you have confirmed that that's what he wanted, not food.

If yours is a multi-cat home divide up the feeding stations, placing one for each cat in each individual's main area of activity. Add an extra one for more choice.

Finally, you can do three things that go nicely together:

• Increase the amount of exercise your cat takes
• Make him 'work' for his food
• Equate feeding with fun

These three actions will help increase the mental stimulation your cat enjoys, and this is an additional aspect of environmental enrichment that is especially useful for indoor cats. You'll come up with your own ideas for your individual cat, but here are some suggestions to consider that will encourage foraging.

• Hide small portions of food in different locations
• Scatter dry diet food around the floor, laying trails of it down hallways or around rooms

- Use commercially produced puzzle feeders or make your own out of small plastic drink bottles
- Use a kitty Kong®
- Make prawn, chicken or liver parcels wrapped in greaseproof or rice paper and tie them to the line of a fishing rod toy, then allow your pet to 'catch and kill' the goodies from time to time to avoid frustration

You can also encourage greater activity by playing hunt the biscuit. Hide treats in different places – under tiny clean plantpots, wrapped in tissue paper inside cardboard tubes (avoid coloured paper and printed cardboard – the dyes may contain toxic heavy metals), in small boxes with holes cut in them – and place them on all the steps up your staircase or on the different levels of your cat gym.

Such activities also provide a useful means of bonding in a non-intrusive way with a timid or newly introduced pet, and they are also a way for little children to interact safely with a cat.

Left: If you are unsure what your cat is demanding from you, try grooming, petting or playing with your cat, rather than automatically feeding him.

Right: Abandoning the food bowl and providing your cat with several small portions of food in different locations to encourage foraging is a good way to avoid boredom and help combat obesity.

Feline lower urinary tract disease

This complicated condition, usually known as FLUTD, probably affects more cats than we realize. Diagnosis isn't straightforward, but specialists are certain that many cases are idiopathic (that is, we can't identify the cause) and that feline idiopathic cystitis (FIC) is stress linked. Hence the importance of understanding your cat's needs and getting things right.

THE SIGNS

This is one of a growing number of conditions where veterinarians and behaviourists work together to treat the problem, which is often only identified through a change in a pet's behaviour. The condition FIC involves a complex relationship between the bladder and the nerves supplying it. It's painful, so some affected pets over-groom their bellies and inner thighs, creating characteristic hair loss patterns. Others pass small quantities of urine in unusual places because of intense bladder irritation or because they associate pain when urinating with the litter tray, outdoor latrine facilities or the last place they went. Consequently, this inappropriate urination moves around the house, to the understandable wrath of owners, whose reaction worsens the cat's condition.

WHO'S AT RISK?

Male and female cats with anxious personalities are susceptible to developing this problem, which seems to affect black and white and Persians cats disproportionately. Those most likely to suffer are cats that are:

- Fed a dry diet
- Inclined to drink insufficient fluid
- Middle-aged
- Overweight
- Inactive
- Kept indoors all the time
- Resident in a multi-cat household

Poorly socialized cats and those that internalize emotional strain rather than responding actively are likely to suffer, as are those unable to reduce their stress levels. It is actually chronic (continuing, unrelieved) stress, rather than acute anxiety, that seems to underlie the problem, although often a recent stressful incident can be identified. Moving house, social upheaval involving owners or other pets, inclement weather that makes going outside to relieve themselves unpleasant and even a change of litter type, have all been identified as precipitating causes. It is, however, a mistake to look at this aspect and miss the overall environmental and social conditions that predispose a cat to developing the problem. An owner's failure to see the wider picture can mean that suffering cats don't get the sort of help they really need.

DIAGNOSIS AND TREATMENT

There is no specific test for FIC. It's diagnosis depends upon ruling out other causes of FLUTD, such as infections, stones or tumours by the use of urine tests, X-rays and ultrasound. Treatment aims to protect the lining of

the bladder, reduce inflammation and relieve pain. Then it's vital to deal with contributory stressors, or the whole process will start again.

HOW CAN WE HELP?

A behavioural programme requires in-depth analysis of all aspects of an affected pet's life, and the therapist will look at:

- The cat's socialization history – were his early experiences too limited or too stressful?
- Genetic inheritance – was he a 'rescued' feral kitten?

Then the therapist will assess the cat's current circumstances:

- Are too many people coming and going in the household for the cat's comfort?
- Does the environment provide adequately for all the cat's natural needs, especially being able to hide and defuse stress?
- Is this a multi-cat home that lacks sufficient facilities for all the cats to have easy access to all the resources?
- Is the cat intimidated inside or outside his home by other cats?

Once all the contributory stressors have been identified, an individual behavioural modification programme is devised. The behaviourist will use a combination of their increased understanding, environmental

enrichment and alterations in styles of interaction with the aim of helping an affected cat cope better with his life. Obviously, however, it's always preferable to prevent the problem developing in the first place.

Above: Some cats, such as black and white breeds, are at higher risk of developing FLUTD than others. Identifying them can help us reduce their exposure to contributory factors.

Left: Persian cats and overweight cats have also been identified as being susceptible to suffering from FLUTD.

EVERYDAY HAPPENINGS AND SPECIAL EVENTS

Changes in your cat's world, such as modifications to the layout of his home, an increase in noise levels, the introduction of new and different smells or alterations in the social composition of his environment, have the potential to upset his emotional equilibrium. Such disturbances may be temporary, with your cat quickly adapting to the new situation, but long-term changes might mean that he struggles to regain his equilibrium, and it is in such circumstances that problem behaviour most often arises. However, many of the difficulties that result are preventable with a little care, and we must pay attention to providing suitable conditions to help him cope if he cannot take the disruption in his stride.

De-stressing your cat

We love our cats, but we also enjoy being with other people and, possibly, other pets. We have hobbies and pastimes, and most of us have jobs that take us out of the home. However, we usually have a choice about what we do and where and when we do it. Our pets, including our cats, have no such luxury. They must take the rough with the smooth and cope as best they can.

Sometimes they find life difficult

It's too easy for owners to remain unaware of, or completely overlook, the impact on their cats of the everyday comings and goings in their lives. The effects of our daily routine will obviously be especially profound with cats that are kept indoors, particularly those that already share a smallish space with others of their own kind to whom they're not related.

You must be alert to the fact that stress and distress are at the heart of many feline problems, and we owe it to our cats to do all we can to prevent the circumstances that cause such problems to arise but also to identify the symptoms and to deal swiftly and effectively with them if they do. For example:

- If your cat quietly withdraws into himself (which happens more than people think) it's easy to assume all is well.
- If your cat suffers from low-grade or even clinical conditions, such as over-grooming or cystitis, they might well be caused by an unrecognized emotional component rather than by an infection.
- If your cat begins to respond overtly do not misinterpret his behaviour as something amusing; some aggressive cats and those with compulsive disorders may be reacting to stress.

Everyday events can be stressful

Household routines help us to manage our responsibilities and domestic chores, but in concentrating on our busy lives

Left: Hiding in bags or under the furniture may look endearing, but it can be a sign that your pet is stressed and frightened. By understanding the signals you can try to help your cat to cope with the cause.

Right: Even young kittens will become attached to favourite sleeping places and blankets, leaving reassuring scents.

it's easy to neglect our cats, however unintentionally. The greatest asset you have in keeping your cat happy is your ability to view everything that happens in his home – and his territory outside it – from his perspective.

Take time to interpret the potential effect of any change on him before it actually happens so that you combine an awareness and understanding of your cat's natural tendencies, your knowledge of his particular sensitivities and a willingness to adapt your environment in order to accommodate them.

Reducing the effects of stress

If your cat seems to be suffering from stress there are three main areas in which you can take steps to reduce if not altogether eliminate its causes. These are when you carry out everyday activities inside your household, when you have some unusual disruption in your home, such as decorating or building work, and disturbance outdoors, which can have an impact even on indoor cats that never go outside.

Inside your home

There are several easy strategies to adopt to avoid upsetting your cat during your daily activities.

- Remove your cat from a room or area before any vacuum cleaning, drilling or hammering or before you make any other noise that's potentially frightening.
- Don't clean all his reassuring marks off skirting (base) boards, furniture, kitchen units and so on because they make him feel secure.
- Don't wash his bed and bedding and favourite blankets and sweaters all at the same time. Rotate the laundry to leave him something that smells comforting and familiar.
- Take especial care if you visit cat-owning friends because when you come home smelling of their pets, your cat will think that other cats have invaded his core area.
- Keep your cat's weekend routines as much like his weekday routine as possible because radical changes in feeding times, play sessions and opportunities for rest and sleep may unsettle him.
- When you bring home shopping, suitcases, briefcases, sports bags, golf trolleys or buggies remember that they will introduce 'foreign' scents that could upset your pet and put them in a closed room or cupboard, especially if your cat has an indoor life. Alternatively, keep an old towel or blanket that he's recently slept on so it smells reassuringly of him and throw it over anything new or newly returned.

During less common household events

Moving furniture disrupts the physical layout of a home, and moving just one item may be enough to start an indoor cat spraying in stress. This doesn't mean that you should never alter anything in your home, of course, but it does mean that when you do you must provide some coping strategies for your cat.

Decorating and refurbishment turn everything upside down as well as introducing unpleasant odours that tend to linger. In the process of decorating all the familiar scent marks your cat had placed around his environment to make it feel like home will be obliterated. Redecorating will be a source of significant stress for many cats, and indoor-only cats have a particularly difficult time. Proceed in a step-by-step fashion, at each stage setting aside a well-supplied sanctuary that will help preserve continuity. As a last resort, consider sending your cat to a cattery while your house is redecorated and then making your home as familiar and cat-friendly as possible again before re-introducing him.

Building work is similarly stressful, especially if you are planning large-scale, noisy projects, such as those involving demolition or tile cutting. It can be immensely disturbing if your cat's outside area is affected as well as his indoor space. It's too easy to underestimate the negative emotional impact of strangers intruding into his territory, especially when it is combined with all the turmoil in the physical, scent and noise aspects of his world.

Having guests to stay can be another stressor for our cats. It can be helpful to ask visitors before they arrive to let you have an old item of clothing they've worn next to their skin so that it's rich in their scent. Offering it to your cat with his favourite food treat or game will help to create positive associations ahead of their arrival. Remember that visitors will bring their own possessions with them, and these can be upsetting, especially if they also own pets. Try to stop them leaving their belongings around in your cat's territory and quickly put them away in the guest room to minimize any stress that disruption in his core area will cause.

Outside your home

Disturbance outside the home can even be unsettling for indoor cats if they are not free to wander away from the disruption to a safe corner, but outdoors cats will be especially stressed by unusual and unexpected events outside the household and some of the greatest sources of stress are other cats.

Strange cats that move in to neighbouring properties may compete with your cat for his territory. The new scents can even be wafted indoors through open doors and windows, and there is the increased risk that every time your cat looks through a window he will see another cat. Never encourage neighbouring cats into your cat's territory, particularly your home, and be careful about leaving garden doors open that provide easy access.

If your cat tends to be intimidated by other cats, make your garden as difficult for them to get into as possible. Increase the height of fences and top them with flimsy trellis or plastic drainpipes that are smooth and difficult to walk along. Make sure that you block up access holes along the base of hedges and fences.

If strange cats like to sit on your shed or garage roof or on the tops of walls, make them uncomfortable with spiky plastic door matting, but make sure that you never, ever use anything that could cause injury.

Remember that indoor cats can be distressed by being overlooked by intruding felines when they are in a conservatory or near the patio doors. If you can, try to break up your cat's view of others and provide him with a small screen to hid behind.

Fireworks and storms can profoundly affect cats, especially in minimalist homes or where outside areas provide little or no sound-absorbing hiding places for cats caught outside. If you have warning, get your cat indoors if he's outside and then close your curtains to minimize the impact of noise, flashes and vibrations. Make sure that your cat has ready access to dark and cosy hiding places and never try to keep him in a room that is largely constructed of glass and contains few noise-absorbent surfaces. Increasing numbers of pets are developing phobias to sound as a result of such experiences.

Right: An indoor cat may be disturbed by the sights and sounds of other cats that he can see through the window.

Well-meaning strangers

Most of us enjoy having visitors to our home, and if we are cat lovers, it's likely that our friends and family members will also like cats. Unfortunately, unthinking cat enthusiasts tend to be somewhat indiscriminate when they are bestowing their affections on any unwary cat that hoves into view, and this is not necessarily a recipe for feline happiness.

Above: Hands-off interactive toys provide an ideal means of bonding shy or unfamiliar cats to visitors – so long as the cats don't just want to hide!

Right: An enclosed, comfy bed is an ideal retreat for a shy or timid cat and has the added advantage of being portable so that it can be moved to a quiet spot when visitors arrive.

Protect your cat

It's not always easy to protect your cat from the intrusive attentions of well-meaning cat lovers. The degree to which you have to intervene and the firmness with which you have to leap between visitor and cat will, of course, depend on the personalities of those involved, but you certainly owe it to your cat to do so. Not only could the stress of imposed unwanted attentions start to undermine your own relationships with your cat, but if he is pursued with too much ardour he may eventually react with uncharacteristic aggression, putting the visitor at risk.

Close scrutiny from a stranger can be particularly distressing for a cat that has been only recently introduced to a home and is not yet completely settled, but it can also upset naturally timid animals or those whose early lives did not predispose them to enjoy close contact with humans.

During social interactions

If you have visitors in your home there are several ways in which you can protect your cat. Be particularly sensitive when your visitors are unfamiliar to your cat by virtue of age, sex or appearance. Even if he's generally bold, monitor their initial contact with each other in case your guests' unfamiliarity unsettles your cat, leading him to behave uncharacteristically unsociably. This is especially important with very young children.

- Don't let a guest impose unwanted attention on your cat.
- Never let anyone pursue him if he runs away, tries to jump out of reach or hides under furniture.
- If you have a kitten, make sure guests don't overtire him because he needs to sleep when he wants to.
- Watch how noisy gatherings affect your pet and make sure that the areas where people congregate don't interfere with his ability to escape or have access to his facilities.

Shrewd moves

If your cat is easily stressed by strangers the obvious solution is to make sure that there are lots of hiding places so that he can simply put himself out of reach and watch what's going on, if he wants to. Alert your guests to the importance of taking things steadily and explain that your cat is more likely to respond positively if they go slowly – otherwise all they'll probably ever see is his retreating tail, because cats can have long memories when negative associations are firmly formed.

If your guests are going to be regularly in your home, make an effort to introduce them properly and slowly to your cat. It can be helpful to have some 'hands-off' toys of the sort your cat likes close by. Give your visitor a fishing rod toy, a handful of wine bottle corks or mouse toys to roll or toss gently towards your cat's hiding place. This allows your cat to retain control, coming out if he wants to or remaining at a comfortable distance if he prefers.

If yours is a multi-cat home, steer your guests towards interaction with your bolder cat rather than persisting with their unwanted attempts to 'bring the shy one out of himself', as some misguided people often want to do.

COPING STRATEGIES
Creating a safe sanctuary in a quiet spare room, study or perhaps your bedroom, if that's where your cat likes to be, will help him cope with all manner of stressful events.

- Set up a miniature indoor environment that caters adequately for all his normal behavioural needs.
- Make sure that you locate everything appropriately, particularly his feeding and latrine facilities.
- Give him as many familiar things as possible to preserve continuity.
- Use commercially available pheromone products to help allay his anxiety (see page 52).

Special events

As we have seen, cats are susceptible to many stress-related conditions, and the best way of avoiding these is to develop an understanding of cats' natural behaviour and learn how our own cat's traits have been shaped by these inherent characteristics. Then we can anticipate and plan for the sort of upheavals that could negatively affect the cat or cats that share our lives.

Above: Some cats enjoy Christmas as much as their owners, others though find it a stressful time of disrupted routines and territorial invasion.

Right: By familiarizing your cat with his pet carrier at an early age you can help to reduce the stress of journeys to the vets or cattery.

Celebrations

We often have parties, sometimes involving fireworks or loud noises, like crackers, when we are celebrating, and although we will be enjoying ourselves, our cats will not, especially when our hectic preparations:

• Encroach on their space
• Make a lot of noise
• Deny them access to areas, such as guest rooms, that are their customary refuges

Such events are worse for indoor cats, but even cats that have access to outdoors will be affected, especially if the weather is bad or if the festivities include fireworks.

You must think about your cat while you are making the arrangements for the party. If you cannot set aside a sanctuary, you might even have to think about sending your cat away to a cattery for the duration.

Journeys, short and long

Whether a trip is long or short, problems for both cat and owner often start with the pet carrier. This is usually because it only appears before visits to the vet, stays in a cattery or moving home – all potentially negative experiences from your cat's point of view. If your cat has endured many such trips during his life and they have been particularly unpleasant or if your cat is especially timid, just approaching the cupboard where the carrier is can be a sufficiently potent signal to send your cat's stress levels through the roof.

A happier and easy alternative is to use the carrier as your cat's bed and refuge all the time:

• Take off the top or door
• Put a favourite blanket inside
• Lay a trail of cat treats leading up to and into it
• Feed him nearby
• Encourage him to play in the vicinity

If you do this often enough he will come to regard the carrier in a more positive light, and you will have helped him find travelling less stressful than he might otherwise do.

The actual trip

On the day itself you can make his confinement more reassuring by rubbing his own social scents from a facial cloth (see page 143) into the corners of his carrier. Alternatively, spray the interior with commercial pheromones, carefully following the manufacturer's instructions. Then, completely cover the basket or box because cats de-stress more quickly in the dark, making sure, of course, that there is good ventilation. Take care not to let him overheat if ambient temperatures are high.

Whatever mode of transport you use, make sure his container is securely tethered and then:

• Convey him with care
• Try to travel when it's quiet, there's less traffic and reduced likelihood of hold-ups
• On longer journeys allow him opportunities to stretch his legs, relieve himself, eat and drink – it's especially important to prevent dehydration

Set out with all the necessary equipment, and never take chances with your pet's physical safety. Cats are easily lost from vehicles, and in strange locations it can be difficult to reunite owner and pet. Then, when you reach your destination, let him settle quietly for a while before you take him out of the carrier.

INSIDE THE CARRIER
When your cat is actually inside his carrier you must make sure that you:

• Prevent him from sliding about by anchoring his blanket
• Minimize noise
• Reduce light levels
• Stop the world intruding, especially when you are going to the cattery or veterinary clinic, where your cat may come face to face with other cats or, worse, dogs

Remember that your cat is trapped in his carrier, and most cats find that an extremely stressful experience.

Going to the vet

Your cat may be one of the lucky 'kitten kindergarten' generation for which appointments with the veterinarian mean fun (see page 89). If he is not, there are a number of things you can do to help minimize the stress that so often accompanies such visits and the difficult period in the waiting room.

Reducing stress

Taking care with the travelling arrangements (see pages 138–9) is only the first step to making visits to the clinic tolerable for your cat. Also bear the following in mind:

- Before your visit do tell the staff about any special needs your pet may have.
- If you arrive hot and bothered, it's bound to be a downhill experience from there. Try to keep calm, have his previous notes and details to hand and make a note of everything you want to discuss.
- Never be tempted to open the basket to cuddle or fuss your cat. He may behave uncharacteristically and make a dash for freedom. He's best left to settle down before the appointment.
- Talk quietly in a monotonous tone to reassure him.
- Put something familiar on the consulting room table for him to sit on.
- If your vet allows it, offer high-value food treats during routine visits to try and build up positive associations.

After the check-up, if you have to wait for medication to be dispensed, think about popping your cat into the car if it's safe and convenient so that he can settle down in the quiet rather than in the bustle and noise of the waiting area. When you get home from the veterinarian never hassle your cat, especially if you're upset and worried. Instead, allow him to settle down as if nothing's actually happened.

Hospitalization

Your cat might have to go to hospital on a day-care basis or for a longer stay if his condition is more serious. The principles are the same:

- Leave something that smells reassuring, but make sure it's old so that you can throw it away if it gets soiled.
- Ask your clinician's advice to see if settling him yourself would be helpful.
- Visit him when you're allowed and keep 'topping' up those familiar odours to maintain his bonds with you and home by taking in something new every day.
- Try to participate in his care – with home-prepared, tempting food treats, for example – but always ask the staff before you offer food or open his cage.

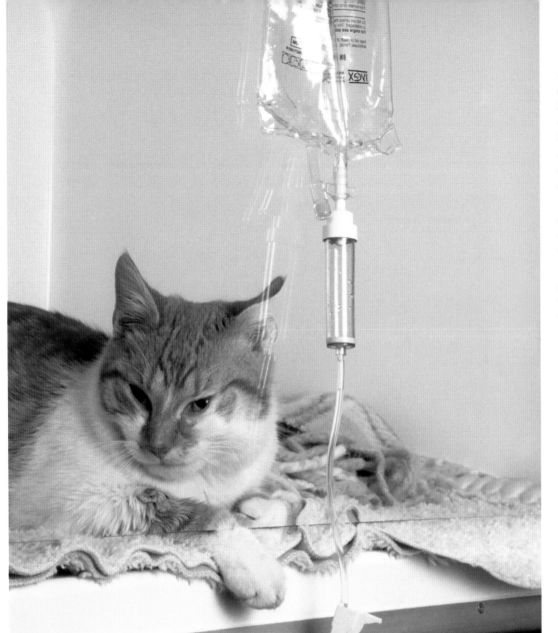

Left: A hospital stay can be stressful for cats and their owners but a few home comforts can make a morale boasting difference.

Far left: Try to reduce the stress of journeys to the vets by giving your cat a familiar blanket or piece of bedding to lie on.

PESTER POWER
Never pester your cat, especially if he's really poorly or in pain. If you put your emotional needs before his, he may come to view you as someone he'd rather not be near when he gets home again.

Back home

After a stay in a vet hospital conduct re-introductions with great care, particularly if your cat has been away some time or has had a difficult time. Whether yours is a single-person household, a large family or a multi-pet home, set aside a sanctuary, allow your cat to settle in and to get up and about in his own time. You must allow him to be in control even if that means keeping some family members, with two or four legs, away from him for a few days.

After especially long stays in hospital it might even be necessary to do a full-scale re-introduction, as if the cat were a new addition to the household, and this is especially true if there was any tension at all in his previous relationships with other pets in the house, including in multi-cat homes, where a cat that smells strange and clinical is a not uncommon cause of a complete breakdown in relations. In these circumstances even cats that had been well bonded for years sometimes react badly to each other. Anticipation, planning and sensitive handling are the key to success.

Finally, always follow your veterinarian's orders and ask for help if you have any concerns. It is better to be regarded as a fusspot than let your pet down.

Holidays and catteries

A frequent conundrum for cat owners is what to do when holidays approach. Do you take your pet with you if you can, send him to a cattery or rely on the services of a sitter, friend or family member? Situations vary, but knowing your cat is crucial in your decision.

Above: *Cats can pay a high price emotionally if owners fail to consider their needs when they all move home.*

Right: *The safe, secure environment of a cattery is a sensible option if your cat is likely to suffer anxiety from the inevitable disruption of his home territory during a house move.*

What to do for the best

If you are planning a long absence on which your cat could accompany you, you might be tempted to take him, but remember that this will involve your cat vacating his outdoor territory. On his return he will have to start re-establishing his 'rights' all over again, which can be a stressful business.

If you have a markedly territorial cat, staying at home will be best, and ideally a close friend or family member can move in to your home during your absence to look after him.

A cattery can be the best solution for any cat that really values human company. Choose with care, asking the advice of cat-owning friends and your veterinarian and making sure that you have had a look round the premises beforehand.

Minimizing stress through familiarity

While you and your cat are separated, you can help minimize his stress by making sure that he has lots of familiar things around him and that his routine is maintained as far as possible. There are several 'stress-busting' measures you can take for veterinary stays, holidays, moving house and other difficult times, such as bereavements or favourite people leaving home. Cats like predictability, so anything you can do to keep routines going as normal is good.

- Structuring mealtimes, menus, play sessions and litter tray hygiene so that little changes in your absence will have a beneficial effect on your cat's morale.
- Make sure your cat has enough appropriately located facilities to provide choice and a sense of being in control.
- Provide your cat with personal space and make sure that no one intrudes into it.

One of the best ways of maintaining normality is by using scent. Give your cat something that smells as if it's his. Blankets, towels, cardboard boxes and dishes all serve this purpose, so don't rush to wash or clean them unless hygiene really does dictate that you do so.

You can also offer your cat a steady supply of scent-impregnated articles from people or other pets he's bonded to. Prepare these in advance, and send your cat on holiday or to hospital with pieces of old clothing, such as T-shirts you've worn but not laundered, and sheets or towels. Seal them in plastic bags so that he can be given a new comforter when the scent has vanished from the old one. He's less likely to snub you when you're reunited if this vital link is maintained while you're apart.

Gently rub his face with squares of soft cotton to pick up the scents he deposits when bunting. Preserve these in plastic bags, then rub them at cat height on new furniture, around a new home, on the legs of unfamiliar people and so on. This will help makes things seem less new and alarming.

Your cat can be unnerved and unsettled at any time by changes in the home – if you move the furniture around, for example, give him time to investigate and find out that the table that used to smell of him still does so. When you buy new items or if you are bringing your cat home after an absence, throw something that smells of him and home over them to mask their foreign aromas. This is especially helpful to indoor cats that get accustomed to having everything in their home exactly as they like it and will become disturbed when something changes.

Always use gradual introduction procedures, even when he or you are returning to an established base. Your cat's social relationships and his relationships with his territory and objects, large and small, within it must always be sensitively handled so that your cat feels that he's the one in control.

Moving home

This can be one of the most stressful events for both cat and owner. The same advice for taking your cat on holiday or to a cattery applies to introducing him to a new home, but there are all kinds of other implications to consider.

Packing can be particularly upsetting, so minimize its impact by restricting your cat's access to areas of upheaval, boxes and cases. Some cats might even be happier and safer in their usual cattery throughout the moving process, when doors and windows might be left open and there will be strangers in the house moving furniture and unplumbing washing machines. Make sure you keep some towels or clothes that are imprinted with your cat's scent so that when you introduce him to his new home there is something familiar to welcome him.

Expanding your household

Cat owners are no different from other people in that they will live, love, set up home together, have children or perhaps even take in lodgers. In their happiness and optimism it's not unusual for people to assume that their cat will be as thrilled as they are when their social group expands, and it's often the case that until the cat develops an irritating habit no one realizes that he is struggling with some aspect of his life.

Adopting other pets

One of the most upsetting events for cats is when different sets of pets are amalgamated, as happens when people with their own pets start living together or get married. When two households become one, it can be that one cat's territory is suddenly 'invaded' by strangers, both human and feline, or, possibly, both households move into a completely new home. Unless this change is handled sensitively, neither option bodes well for your cat's happiness, and this is especially true where multi-cat groups are involved.

Making it work

When you are introducing a cat to a new home where there is an already-established cat or cats or whether you are hoping to integrate the much loved cats from two separate households, the procedure's the same.

- Prepare the environment by making sure there are lots of resources and separate facilities for each cat.
- Take your time and never set deadlines or try to impose a timetable.
- Allow each cat to settle into separate areas.
- Use every stress-reducing measure you can – lots of exercise, nice food, unobtrusive human company and calming commercial pheromones (see page 52).
- Create positive associations with the stranger's scent.
- Gradually mix their odours in the environment but monitor their reactions when you do so.

Above all, be realistic and do not expect miracles. Despite all your best efforts some cats are just not destined to accept each other, and it is far better to admit defeat and find another solution, possibly even re-homing one or more of the cats, than to let them all suffer.

Right: Anticipation and careful planning are usually the key to successful expansion of any household's social group.

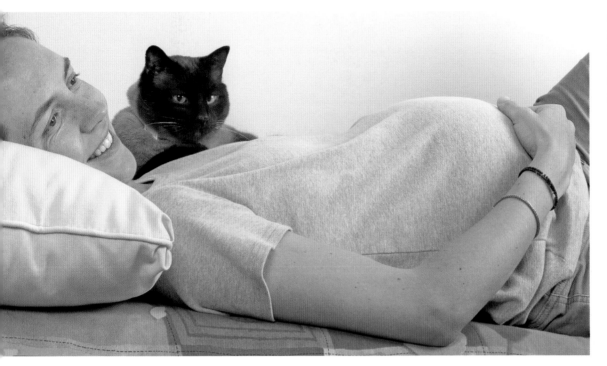

Dogs

Early socialization experiences can make a huge difference if you ever have to introduce a dog into your previously cat-only household. It will also help enormously if your cat has been used to living with another species, but success really hinges on individual personalities, supervision, good canine control and careful amalgamation. Never rush things and make sure that your cat retains control over his territory for as long as he needs to, which might mean keeping the dog out of a room in which the cat has established a retreat. You'll also need a fair amount of luck.

Two-legged additions

Probably the most exciting event in any home is the arrival of children. A new baby will turn your life upside down, and it will also alter everything in your cat's world.

- The expectant mother who used to be out at work is suddenly at home all day.
- Strange-smelling furnishings, clothing and toiletries appear, altering the environmental layout and familiar scent profile of the home.
- The nursery, which used, particularly in small properties, to be the room where your cat liked to sit in the sun or hide from visitors, is suddenly out of bounds, which causes him frustration.
- Contact between your cat and you becomes erratic and even spasmodic.

Then, worst of all from your cat's point of view, a small being, who looks, smells and sounds different from anything that most cats have ever encountered invades the territory, absorbing all the attention previously lavished on the cat and upsetting the daily routines. Horror of horrors, this newcomer appears to be a permanent addition to the home.

Plan ahead

You will have a hundred other things to think about, but it's important to prepare your cat for the changes that are going to take place in your and his life. If your cat wasn't socialized with babies and children make every effort to improve the deficiencies before your new baby arrives.

- Invite friends with children to visit. If you make everything as positive as possible for your cat he will come to associate little people with special food and lots of play.
- If you haven't got any suitable friends, buy a good-quality CD of baby noises.
- In good time begin to establish new routines, including some you'll be able to keep up, such as your cat's evening playtime.
- Make the necessary changes to your home gradually, allowing your cat time to adapt.

When the time comes, carry out the introductions slowly and carefully. Don't impose the baby on your cat and don't neglect him, but don't inadvertently stress him by over-compensating. Your cat will adjust best if his established routine is disrupted as little as possible.

Once your baby's on the move, make sure your cat can always be part of your group but has numerous readily accessible options for retreat and quick getaways. Never take chances with the safety of either.

PROBLEM BEHAVIOUR

By now you will know your cat well, and you will no doubt also have identified a number of areas where, as an owner, you might have got things wrong. You might have unrealistic expectations of your cat or have adopted 'it'll be all right' attitudes that fail to properly prepare for or address signs that things are far from all right in your cat's world. You might have placed inadvertent pressure on your cat or failed to comprehend the impact of everyday events, not to mention the life-changing experiences that even we have difficulty adjusting to. All this can upset your cat's emotional stability and lead to problem behaviour. In addition, some medical conditions can have a harmful effect on behaviour, causing problems that can strain the owner–cat bond. This is why it's always essential to rule out or deal with any such issues before embarking on the quest to resolve the problem behaviour.

Problems, what problems?

Defining problem behaviour might seem easy. Some conditions, including compulsive disorders that cause cats to damage themselves, are clearly problematic, but others, such as stropping that damages furniture, which is definitely a problem for owners, is all too appropriate in the light of natural feline behaviour.

When things go wrong

As an owner, your negative response to your cat's problem behaviour will often make matters worse. If you are irritated and annoyed by something your cat does, he will be aware of your feelings and this will make him feel even more stressed. He might then develop different behavioural problems – indoor urinary spraying, for example or over-grooming – because he is trying to reassure himself that everything in his life is all right.

Some problems are, of course, fairly straightforward to recognize and deal with, but it would be a mistake to look at the surface only. It is far better for you to examine every aspect of an affected cat's life and all facets of his behaviour to find the issues.

Motivation is key

When you are trying to understand your cat's behavioural problems you need to search for the motivation underlying the difficulties you have identified. This may be obvious but equally it might take some investigation to identify. There may even be more than one motivation associated with a particular issue, and it could change over time. It's important to be alert to all possible contributing causes or you might fail in your diagnosis and in the solutions you adopt.

A good illustration of potential pitfalls is FIC (see pages 128–9), which is a stress-related condition. The condition is also painful, and the pain is usually associated with the litter tray or the last place your cat relieved himself. The typical pattern with the condition, therefore, is of urination all over the house as your cat attempts to get away from what he perceives to be the source of the pain. Owners who do not understand what's happening, get angry and frustrated when they find that carpets and bedding have been soiled, and their reaction causes further distress to the cat. A vicious cycle ensues, and the problem doesn't get better.

Golden rules of diagnosis

There are a few guidelines that can help you help your cat. The most important of these is to keep calm. Never punish your cat or withdraw your affection. Your cat won't understand why you've changed, and if environmental issues or stress underlie his problems, they're only likely to get worse.

Remember, too, that cats don't share our values. They are never nasty, spiteful or deceitful – but they're never grateful either.

- Watch your cat and observe his behaviour in the light of what you know about normal feline characteristics and traits.
- Consider your pet's genetic inheritance, socialization experiences and life history. Often, we can see why a cat is behaving as he is now, when we understand who he is and what he's learned about living with people, in a home and with others animals, both indoors and outside.
- Try to determine when the problem began. What was happening in your cat's world at the time? Was there a major and obvious stressor that upset your cat, or has there been a series of subtle, unrecognized pressures that ultimately became too much for him?
- What's happened since? Have your reactions made things worse or better and can you work out why? This is especially relevant if the problem behaviour is intermittent. Considering your cat's situation when all is well could help you find the solution to what happens when the problem is apparent.

Left: *Stealing food from your plate can be seen as a response to your cat's ancestral instincts to capture and eat prey, not as a major behavioural problem. Avoid giving him the opportunity.*

Right: *While kitten antics are entertaining, don't encourage this behaviour as it may continue into adulthood with disastrous consequences for pet and home alike.*

Individual problems

If you are having difficulties with your cat's behaviour you might already have worked out the cause and what you should do. It's often reassuring to know that you're not alone and that numerous other cat lovers have been in the same position. The behavioural problem that no owner wants is the one that no one has ever encountered before.

House soiling

This is a common problem, but don't make the mistake of just looking at the behaviour. Remember to examine everything that has an effect on your cat, starting with an examination of the available toileting facilities and how satisfactory they are – not from our point of view, but from your cat's. If you live in a multi-cat home, you need to look at each cat's facilities.

- Keep a diary and a plan of the affected locations; this will often help you identify what is causing the problem.
- Distinguish between inappropriate elimination and scent marking by looking at precisely what happens, where and when. Remember that sometimes both occur together.
- Relate your cat's behaviour to that of the other pets and people. It could be that what you provide is fine but that another member of the household, human, feline or canine, is stopping him getting to his facilities.

When you have identified the problem, rectify any deficiencies, such as access, cleanliness and privacy, and deal with contributing social issues by providing something else for your other cat or cats to do.

Aggression

Cats often show aggression – sometimes it's aimed at people, sometimes at other cats or dogs – and generally it's normal and not intended to be nasty. That doesn't mean that aggressive behaviour should be ignored, but you should make an effort to understand rather than chastise your cat if the aggression becomes more than the occasional reaction to an immediately identifiable cause, such as a visit to the house by a strange dog. Confrontation with an habitually aggressive cat will not only make things worse but could put people at risk.

It's important to work out why your cat is being aggressive and help him deal effectively with the causes so that he no longer needs to react in this way. Sometimes your cat's reaction will be the result of fear, which might be the result of poor socialization or a frightening, possibly painful, experience. In a multi-cat home the aggression can arise because the cat is having to compete for essential resources. Check that his access to food and the catflap or litter tray is unimpeded. In a small home, with few hiding places and limited space for the facilities, your cat might become aggressive because he feels that he cannot control his life.

Ask yourself if unrealistic expectations of what your cat can cope with in his environment and social group are undermining his emotional equilibrium, making him touchy and self-defensive. Enriching the environment, providing separate territories for individual cats and reducing inadvertent pressure within human–cat relationships can often hold the key to success.

Predatory behaviour

All cats require appropriate outlets for their inborn predatory instincts, and if these are lacking in his home your cat might well try to find his own, inappropriate, often potentially dangerous, outlets as he lies in wait for unwary feline companions, passing human ankles or a wagging canine tail to sink his claws and teeth into.

The best way to overcome this type of unwelcome behaviour is to provide:

- A complex, stimulating environment and plenty of different exercise facilities
- Lots of cat-friendly toys, especially those that provide safe opportunities for stalking, pouncing, catching and tearing

In addition, it's important to make sure that this type of behaviour never gets any human response that could inadvertently be construed by the cat as rewarding. Your cat will think that a shrieking, erratically moving 'victim' is entirely natural. Wearing thick, protective clothes and boots indoors may seem eccentric, but by making yourself an unrewarding target you will quickly become unattractive prey. Your other pets will need a different type of help on this score.

Frustration

If your cat feels frustrated he might manifest his stress by being aggressive (see above). The cause of his behaviour might lie in his past – perhaps your pampered kitten didn't learn to cope with being denied what he wanted – or his present circumstances might lead to inappropriate outpourings of arousal, with its potential to harm others. Again, identifying the cause, rectifying deficiencies and altering styles of handling and interaction are crucial.

Anxiety and stress

Fear, anxiety and stress commonly go hand in hand. These emotional states can have a serious negative impact on the wellbeing of afflicted cats by affecting their quality of life and undermining their relationships with others, owners included. Sadly, this suffering is not always obvious, especially if your cat has simply withdrawn into himself, rather like a depressed person.

HOW CAN YOU HELP?

In order to help your cat you need to remember everything you've learned about a cat's normal behaviour and how it relates to the instinctive traits that he has inherited from his distant forebears. With this in mind, consider:

- The importance of good socialization and habituation (see pages 86–7).
- The need to have realistic expectations of each cat in terms of his genetic inheritance, individual temperament and life history.
- The provision of an adequate, interesting environment that doesn't cause distress and that contains everything your cat needs to adopt his natural coping strategies.
- The significance of sensitive handling and, perhaps, the necessity to modify the emotional demands you place on your cat.
- The need to anticipate and plan for major and minor stressors.
- The readiness to offer extra help and protection at potentially troublesome times.

These strategies should give you all the tools you will need to identify any special behavioural needs your cat has and then to set about addressing them in a constructive way.

If, however, despite your best efforts, both you and your cat find that you're out of your respective depths, consult your veterinarian to double-check that you haven't overlooked a medical problem. If your vet gives the all-clear, ask for a referral to a properly qualified feline behaviourist, who will be able to offer specialist help.

COMPULSIVE DISORDERS

There is one category of feline stress-related behaviours that can have serious welfare consequences. The group includes a range of behaviours that were previously termed stereotypical or obsessive-compulsive. Whether cats have the cognitive abilities required for obsessing is debatable, so now the expression repetitive behaviours or compulsive disorders is preferred. These are good descriptive labels, because the behaviours that fall into this group are, indeed, generally repeated in a way that suggests the affected pet feels compelled to perform them with great intensity, over and over again.

MOTIVATION AND FRUSTRATION

It's not only stress that contributes to the development of these problems. Frustration and motivational conflict, the sort of inner turmoil we're all familiar with, can, if unresolved, result in such behaviour patterns. There may be no obvious eliciting stimulus (trigger); rather a conglomeration of factors – environmental, social and individual – come together to cause such conditions. Frequently, an internal mixture of experience and personality seems to lead to a pet displaying a compulsive behaviour. Genetic influences certainly contribute too, because some breeds are particularly affected, with individual families sometimes disproportionately so.

WHAT DO WE SEE?
There are several types of feline compulsive behaviours, but the following are the most often seen.

Psychogenic alopecia
In this condition, which is also known as over-grooming, hair loss tends to be around the cat's belly and inner thighs. Normal shedding leaves a smooth coat, but these cats often barber, licking frantically, chewing, tugging and pulling out tufts of fur, so that affected areas feel spiky.

Self-mutilation
Some affected cats make frenzied attacks on their own hind ends and tails. Feline orofacial pain syndrome is another compulsive disorder that has only recently been recognized. It is mainly seen in Burmese, but sometimes also affects Siamese, Burmilla and domestic short-haired cats. Afflicted pets lick and chew in an exaggerated way and claw at their mouths. Initially, a dental problem will be the suspected cause, and such conditions warrant an immediate veterinary appointment.

Hyperaesthesia
Cats with this condition, the so-called 'rippling skin syndrome' which is also sometimes referred to as 'twitchy cat disease', suffer from bouts when they seem almost to be hallucinating. Their skin twitches in a rather dramatic way, and they tend to dash about then suddenly freeze. These periods are very different from the normal 'funny five minutes' that many cats have,

especially around mealtimes in the morning and evening.

Pica
Cats can exhibit an abnormal craving for non-food items, which is termed 'Pica'. Siamese and Burmese cats, however, are particulary susceptible to sucking and chewing fabrics like wool.

Above: Cats suffering from hyperaesthesia may appear to freeze suddenly following a bout of activity.

Left: Particular breeds, such as Siamese and Burmese, are prone to chewing or sucking wool and fabrics, a condition known as pica.

The holistic approach

With any apparent compulsive disorder thorough clinical investigation is essential. Like psychogenic alopecia, self-mutilation or the skin twitching of hyperaesthesia, external parasites and FLUTD (see pages 128–9) can result in hair loss and apparent irritation, while Pica is a feature of several organic diseases. The aim is always to rule out or treat medical causes and control pain.

The prognosis

Unfortunately, despite the potential health risks and the harm that some cats inflict upon themselves, compulsive disorders are problem behaviours we find difficult to understand. The biological mechanisms underlying such manifestations of stress, frustration and inner conflict are usually complex, may differ from cat to cat, and may involve the neuro-transmitters in the brain, such as dopamine and serotonin, and the body's own pain relievers, endorphins.

The good news, however, is that our knowledge of these disorders is increasing all the time, and the chances of being able to help cats that suffer from them is improving. Even if it is not possible to cure them entirely, it is still generally possible to help them overcome some of their problem behaviour.

The more we understand our individual cats and their behaviour problems, the better we are able to help them.

The way forward

It is often necessary to embark on a thorough behavioural examination at the same time as clinical tests are being conducted so that precious time is not lost during which the cat's condition worsens. Sometimes no physical abnormality can be detected, so behavioural therapy is the only course of action that can be pursued, although it is often used in combination with medication.

An individual cat's behaviour modification programme will, of course, be based on his personality, life history and circumstances. However, it will be rooted in all we know about:

• Natural feline behaviour
• Environmental enrichment
• The impact on your cat of his social group, styles of interaction and so on

In addition, in some cases the judicial use of psychoactive medication (along the lines of anti-depressants in humans) is recommended, although the range of drugs suitable for cats is much more limited.

It is, of course, much better if compulsive disorders never occurred in the first place, and that is why it's so essential that we apply all the important principles we've learned about the everyday care of our cats.

Can cats be cured?

When it comes to compulsive disorders, 'cure' is a problematic term to use. It's better to talk about 'resolution', because the word cure implies that the problems have been sorted forever. In reality, behavioural therapists can do a lot and return many of these affected cats to 'normal', but if the conditions in which they find themselves change to the detriment of the cat, relapse is all too possible.

The silent sufferers

Compulsive disorders represent fairly extreme manifestations of stress, frustration and motivational conflict. However, they are apparently becoming increasingly prevalent, and this, combined with the significant changes in owner expectations and feline lifestyles in recent years, has given rise to concerns that they are even more common than is realized.

The independent, secretive and solitary nature of our cats' ancestors means that, despite our effects on their behaviour, the pets living with us still don't always draw attention to themselves. Veterinarians and behaviourists are directing more thought than ever towards the 'non-responding' cats: those more passive individuals that simply withdraw emotionally, don't give anyone any trouble but quite possibly suffer low-grade chronic stress that no one picks up on, because, like so much in the feline world, the signs are quiet and subtle. This is undoubtedly an area of increasing importance to all those who are concerned about the welfare of cats, and it is an area to which scientific endeavour will be directed over the coming years.

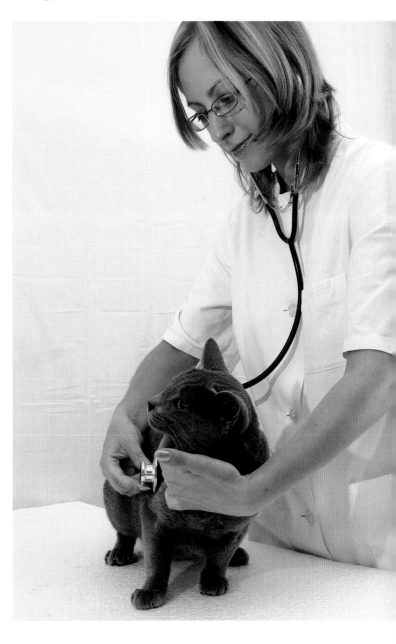

Right: Working together, owners and professionals can do a lot to combat feline problem behaviour.

Left: It is possible that some cats with a passive, quiet nature are suffering from low-grade chronic stress and more advances in understanding behavioural problems may help these silent suffers.

A lighter note

Fortunately, not all feline problems are as distressingly serious as compulsive disorders. Some feline behaviour is potentially risky – chewing plants that are poisonous to cats, both indoors and in the garden, or gnawing electric cables out of frustration or to get their own way – but others are amusing (for a while, at least) and even rather endearing.

Left: It's always worth remembering that some problem behaviours are also rather endearing!

Far left: Having a cat in your home brings much entertainment and comfort, and through understanding their needs a little more, both your lives will benefit.

Attention seeking

Attention-seeking behaviour manifests itself in a variety of different ways. Anything a cat does, no matter how casually, that evokes a satisfying human response is likely to be repeated, possibly even extended, so it pays to think ahead. It may be amusing, for the first few times, when your cat swings from the bottom of your dressing gown first thing in the morning as you rush to the bathroom. It's likely to be less entertaining if the behaviour persists for years and all your long skirts and trousers bear the imprint of teeth and claws.

It is equally important not to laugh or shriek if your bold but bored or stressed Siamese or Burmese starts sucking an old sweater. You might be quite pleased to have an excuse to buy something new, but you'll be less thrilled when the new sweater becomes the favoured target or, more seriously, a woollen intestinal obstruction puts the cat in hospital for major surgery, with a veterinary bill equivalent to the cost of several garments.

Their funny habits are part of the charm of cats. However, we really do owe it to our pets to check everything they do with our knowledge of natural feline behaviour. Then, we can be sure that something apparently innocuous doesn't spring from, or mask, boredom, lack of appropriate facilities and so on. We must also be aware, of course, of seemingly inoffensive incidents that could well become rods for our own back.

Sucking and kneading

Some 'normal but nuisance' habits are so firmly rooted in an individual cat's psyche that no amount of ignoring or distraction can deflect or extinguish them. Such rituals as sucking human hair, ears or necks fall readily into this group. Together with kneading beds, blankets, cushions and human laps, they're just extensions of kittenish behaviour in the nest. During suckling the kittens perform these same actions to encourage their mother to release her milk. With some pets early weaning or the neotenizing effects of neutering may prolong such traits into adulthood, when people simply learn to live with them, even if loving them proves impossible.

And so ...

Cats have lived alongside us for hundreds of years, but never so intimately as now. They have given many, many people enormous pleasure, something they continue to do today. They entertain, amuse and console us, often by just being around. In return, cat lovers derive considerable pleasure in caring and sharing with their feline companions.

Thankfully, the situation seems set to continue, and it appears that increasing numbers of formerly non-cat people are being won over to the side of the cat, something that gives us all the more reason to learn as much as we can about our chosen animal companions.

We owe it to the cats who own us to see the world from their point of view. They may not be able to talk, but the belief that cats cannot tell us how they feel and how they have been affected by what happens to and around them has definitely been laid to rest. We ignore clear indications that they need us to do things differently or help them in a particular way, to their detriment and ours. However, if we use what we've learned so far, strive to increase our knowledge and continue to look, listen and learn from the cats we live with, we'll undoubtedly have richer, happier lives than would otherwise be the case, and more importantly, so will they.

Index

Acknowledgements

Executive Editor Trevor Davis
Project Editor Ruth Wiseall
Design Manager Tokiko Morishima
Designer Ginny Zeal
Production Controller Nigel Reed and Carolin Stransky
Picture Research Giulia Hetherington

Author acknowledgements

I would like to extend my grateful thanks to all those at Hamlyn who worked on this book. It has been both fascinating and rewarding to watch the process by which it has grown and developed. In doing so I have learned a great deal and am filled with admiration for the range of skills and talents they have deployed in transforming a simple written manuscript into something much more. I am particularly indebted to Trevor Davies for giving me this opportunity and to Ruth Wiseall my editor. Their patience in guiding and educating me in what was for me a novel undertaking has been extraordinary and is very much appreciated.

In addition it gives me great pleasure to thank all the colleagues who, both formally and informally, have so generously shared with me their knowledge of all matters feline. Thanks must also go to my family and friends for their support over the last few years, especially in my writing endeavours. Above all I acknowledge my debt to all the cats it has been my privilege to encounter both professionally and personally – they have brought me much pleasure and taught me so much.

Photographic acknowledgements

Alamy/Paul Cox Front Cover; /Ace Stock Limited 73; /Arco Images 29, 33, 65, 99, 124; /Barry L. Runk 114; /Barry Mason 28, 49; /blickwinkel 31, 87; /Bloom Works Inc. 81; /Bob Turner 51; /Brian Hoffman 66; /CN Boon 84; /EP TravelStock 101; /Gari Wyn Williams 23; /Helene Rogers 17; /Isobel Flynn 64, 120, 125; /Jonathan Littlejohn 106; /Juniors Bildarchiv 40, 53, 113, 148; /Jupiterimages/Creatas 146, 150; /KonradZelazowski 137; /Lifestyle Concepts & Emotions 79; /Mark Duffy 94; /Mark Morgan 57; /Mylife photos 145; /Peter Cavanagh 47; /Peter Coombs 52; /Picture Partners 93; /Poligons Photo Index 34; /Rob Walls 132; /Sherab 82, 88; /Superclic 56; /tbkmedia.de 58; /Top-Pics TBK 86; /Webstream 129. Ardea 62, 68, 72, 110, 119, 126, 139, 144, 55, 115, 149; /Francois Gohier 69; /Jean Michel Labat 19, 24, 26, 38, 41, 43, 50, 61, 76, 91, 109; /John Daniels 8, 10, 21, 36, 42, 60, 67, 74, 78; /Kenneth Fink 71.
Art Directors and Trip/Helene Rogers 151.
Corbis UK Ltd/Niall Benvie 111; /Alley Cat Productions/Brand X/ 96; /Carlos Avila Gonzalez 112; /Cynthia Diane Pringle 25; /Jane Burton 95; /Julie Habel 70; /PBNJ Productions 128.
FLPA/Mitsuaki Iwago/Minden Pictures Back Cover.

Getty Images/Jane Burton 107; /Andreas Kuehn 142; /Konrad Wothe/Minden Pictures 20; /Renzo Mancini 135.
istockphoto.com/Denis Tabler 155; /gwmullis 127; /Ira Bachinskaya 154; /Jamie Carroll 77; /Maartje van Caspel 18; /Marcus Lindstr√∂m 48; /Maurice van der Velden 39; /Nicolette Neish 122; /Ricardo Garza 15; /Robyn Glover 6; /schwartz 89; /Shaun Lowe 16; /Trevor Allen 130, 138; /Valentin Casarsa 80.
Jupiterimages/Corbis 156; /Stephen Chiang 153.
Nature Picture Library/Bartussek/ ARCO 90; /De Meester/ARCO 102; /Francois Savigny 12; /Nick Upton 27.
NHPA/Laurie Campbell 59.
Photolibrary 104, 118; /Japack Photo Library 32; /Juniors Bildarchiv 13, 45.
RSPCA Photolibrary 22, 123; /Andrew Forsyth 140, 143; /Angela Hampton 85, 116, 141; /E A Janes 97.
Shutterstock 4; /aceshot 1 92; /Babusi Octavian Florentin 46; /April Turner 30; /Babusi Octavian Florentin 2; /Fernando Jose Vasconcelos Soares 108; /Floris Slooff 103; /Gregory Albertini 136; /J. Helgason 44; /Karl R. Martin 117; /Nicholas Rjabow 35; /Tatiana Morozova 14.
Warren Photographic 100, 152, 157.